# THE GAME'S NOT OVER

# THE GAME'S NOT OVER

||||||||||||||||||||||||||||||||||||||||||||||||||||||||

*In Defense of Football*

||||||||||||||||||||||||||||||||||||||||||||||||||||||||

## GREGG EASTERBROOK

**PUBLIC**AFFAIRS
A Member of the Perseus Books Group

*for Nancy Easterbrook Tatum*

*fiat lux*

# CONTENTS

# CONTENTS

# PREFACE

# *America's Love–Hate Relationship with the NFL*

One evening in May 2015, all three network newscasts led with the same shocking story. The subject wasn't a natural disaster, corruption in politics or war in some distant land. The story all three network newscasts considered the most important development of the day was monkey business in the National Football League.

An NFL-commissioned report had just concluded that before a playoff game occurring in rain, the New England Patriots improperly let air out of footballs. That made the ones clutched by New England players a little easier to hold than those used by the opponent, the Indianapolis Colts.

As kickoff approaches before a game of American-style football—for the rest of this book, just "football"—each side presents a bag of pigskins to the officials for inspection. The purpose of this procedure, in effect down to the high school level, is to prevent the home team from doctoring the visitor's footballs to make them slippery. New England's innovation, according to the report, was to doctor its own footballs.

Those familiar with the gridiron chortled. A few years back, I was football coach of the middle-school affiliate of a large public high school in Maryland, where I live. Before my charges took the field on a rainy day, I called the varsity coach to ask if he had any tips for wet conditions. "Let a little air out of the balls your guys use," the varsity coach advised.

Did I follow this advice? No comment.

It turned out that in the New England-Indianapolis game, the Patriots won by a comfortable margin: the better team, they would have carried the day even if using a bowling ball on offense. But it seemed they'd done something underhanded and been caught. The scandal quickly was dubbed Deflategate, though a columnist proposed PSIcheated as a more elegant name.

The report spelling out details of how the Patriots were said to have cheated became a national sensation, leading to the evening-news emphasis. Compiled by a law firm, the document ran a numbing 243 pages. Included were ninety-four charts or graphs, 127 footnotes, a lengthy disquisition on the Ideal Gas Law and a number of pseudo-precise remarks, such as the note that "ball P6" was not at 12 pounds-per-square-inch, but rather at 11.95 PSI.

Before the report, when word first broke that New England had been caught tampering with footballs, there was a press conference at team headquarters near Boston. Michele Steele of ESPN reported that "100 journalists and at least 30 camera crews" attended—more media attention than has ever been focused on, say, infrastructure renewal or finding a cure for malaria.

At the packed press conference, quarterback Tom Brady—

among the best football players of his generation and leading a charmed life as a wealthy, handsome athlete married to a gorgeous fashion model—stood up to declare, "I have no knowledge of anything." Brady seemed sincere as he insisted upon his innocence. He knew nothing!

The report would conclude that the Patriots' star actively directed the doctoring of the footballs, and his "no knowledge of anything" was a barefaced lie. Brady and Patriots' owner Robert Kraft denied the charge with all the vigor that Luxembourg denies being a tax haven. Patriots' faithful would perceive a vast conspiracy, and don FREE TOM BRADY T-shirts. Later, Brady would tell NFL Commissioner Roger Goodell that just before he was to be questioned on the missing PSI, he destroyed the cell phone he carried during the time the footballs were handled. Brady contended the smashed cell phone had nothing, nothing to do with the controversy.*

---

* Brady said he smashed his previous mobile phone—actually told his personal assistant to smash the old cell—ah, for the life of a millionaire—solely because he longed for the new iPhone 6 model that had arrived in stores.

Though what was happening to Brady when he made his case to Roger Goodell was more like an employee performance review than a courtroom matter, since the issue was later dragged into court, let's apply legal reasoning to the Case of the Smashed Samsung.

When defendants invoke the Fifth Amendment on the stand, juries are forbidden to assume this means the defendant is hiding something. Refusing to testify against yourself is a constitutional right, and rights may be invoked without explanation: conceptually, taking the Fifth reveals nothing other than that the defendant is a U.S. citizen. The rule about destruction of evidence is different. There's no constitutional option to destroy evidence—the evidence is not a citizen and not protected by the Bill of Rights. When someone destroys evidence, judges or juries can assume this was because the evidence was damning. So by telling Jeeves to smash his old phone, Brady essentially admitted the charge against him.

An absurdly drawn-out legalistic melodrama followed: testimony with stenographers present, high-powered law firms Paul, Weiss and Covington & Burling firing all-guns broadsides, and a 456-page transcript that made the 243-page report seem succinct. In September 2015, a federal judge lifted Brady's suspension but came to no conclusion on the cheating charge: perhaps by the time you read this the Supreme Court, the Vatican and the United Nations Security Council have weighed in. Goodell said destruction of the phone went to the "integrity" of the sport—though, in 2007, when Goodell himself received video evidence that the New England Patriots had illegally taped the opponents' sideline, the commissioner immediately destroyed the tapes.

Now here's the rub. The first news of football tampering, leading to the "no knowledge of anything" press conference, broke about a week before the Seattle-New England Super Bowl of 2015.* The NFL report concluding that tampering occurred was not released until well after that contest had been played, with Brady leading the Patriots to a thrilling last-second victory and receiving the Super Bowl MVP award. Had Brady copped to the allegations at the press conference, he might have been suspended for the Super Bowl. By denying everything, Brady came out way ahead.

Whether grown men are chasing footballs that have been properly inflated may seem too trivial to discuss, let alone to activate such a national ruckus. The over-the-top reaction to a

---

* That contest may also be called "the 2014 Super Bowl," because it concluded the 2014 season. Most NFL postseason games fall after January 1, leading to perennial confusion regarding dates. This book will identify games based on the year actually played.

rumor about football air pressure shows the level of American mania for the National Football League. Nothing about the NFL is trivial: for professional football is the most important sport of the most important nation on Earth.

Pro football television ratings crush all other sports combined. Twenty of the twenty most-watched television events in the United States were Super Bowls. Since 2011, NBC's *Sunday Night Football* has been the number-one show on American television—not the number-one athletic event, the number-one show. Since 2006, ESPN's *Monday Night Football* has been the number-one American cable show—not the number-one athletic event, the number-one show. In the ratings, even the NFL draft crushes most other prime-time television. The annual NFL draft is a television juggernaut: millions tune in not to watch pro football being played, but merely being talked about. And the 2015 Super Bowl, amid all the controversy, was the most-watched program in the history of television.

So the obvious reason the PSIcheated scandal struck such a chord was the incredible popularity of all aspects of the NFL. But there was a second, deeper reason: that the National Football League holds up a mirror to American society. Ours is an outsized nation, and in the NFL, the most outsized of athletic leagues, we see our reflection.

In this instance, the doctored-footballs accusation was a reflection of the national suspicion that people who reach positions of power and privilege, whether in sports, business, government, school, or on Wall Street, do so by cheating. Every time a once-respected leader is dragged away in handcuffs—as I write this, criminal charges had just been filed against a former

Speaker of the House of Representatives—the worry increases that corruption is rampant at the top. Who better than Brady, star of a team on the verge of another championship, he of the magazine-cover wife and male-model looks, of riches beyond imagination, to personify our national suspicion of success? What better demonstration than a team caught red-handed on the eve of the biggest event in the history of television?

The litany of concerns Americans see in their league is long—and because we love our football, we fear that all of them reflect on us:

- *Too much violence.* Hollywood glamorizes slaughter and torture in movies that soccer moms take their kids to see at suburban shopping malls. Since the turn of the new century, under presidents Republican and Democratic, the United States has invaded Afghanistan and Iraq, while bombing Libya, Pakistan, Syria and Yemen. In 2015 alone, mass murders occurred in Louisiana, South Carolina, Oklahoma, Tennessee and Texas. America has a tormented relationship with violence—and a violent national sport.
- *Concussions.* In a society increasingly based on education and mental skills, it just can't be good that the national sport extols men who injure each other's heads.
- *Domestic abuse.* Who would have guessed that the NFL could become a women's issue? In 2014, when Baltimore Ravens star Ray Rice knocked his fiancée unconscious, this brought into the open the concern that domestic harm to women too often is covered up.

PREFACE

- *Misuse of public funds.* One reason for rising inequality is that the privileged get better deals than average people. The NFL, with $12 billion annually in revenue, is heavily subsidized by taxpayers, while enjoying antitrust waivers unavailable to small businesses. The NFL's special treatment is based not on merit but on insider access to politicians.

In today's NFL, there's much not to like. There is also a lot that's terrific, creating a love-hate relationship so many Americans feel with the national game.

- Football is a wonderful sport, and quality of play has never been higher. Games are exciting, usually close: every play counts. A well-played NFL contest is aesthetically beautiful. The complex tactics of twenty-two men doing different things on each down make football a living chessboard. After a good NFL game, such as the 2015 New England-Seattle Super Bowl, even the jaded say, "Wow!"
- Professional football represents an artificial universe that a person can become wrapped up in and care deeply about, yet where it makes no difference what happens. In international affairs, economics and race relations, terrible things occur. In the NFL, only entertainment occurs. That can make losing oneself in this artificial universe appealing. As an outlet for emotions, the NFL is hard to beat.
- Pro sports, and especially football, are a place where virtues are rewarded: teamwork, dedication and skill lead to success and fame.

- xv -

- Rooting for the city's NFL team brings people together, which matters in an increasingly polarized, fractious society. Those from all walks of life can join in appreciating art, music, dance or nature too. But the numbers will never be as large as the numbers for pro football.
- Enthusiasm for the NFL cuts across lines of race, income and religion. There aren't many topics on which white and African American, wealthy and poor, and those of every belief system can talk to each other and cheer together. Pro football is one.

Love of the NFL runs deep and broad in American society. I attend way too many football games, including the Super Bowl each year, and can describe in detail the tactics and big plays of numerous contests of the past. I know dozens of men and a not inconsiderable number of women who are the same. From justices to janitors, tens of millions of Americans are addicted to pro football. This craving is found in every demographic, every area of the country, every aspect of our society.

And with good reason. But as the scandals pile one atop the other, we are nagged by a question: Is it okay to like pro football?

This book will argue that in significant aspects, the NFL is broken and needs reform. This book also will argue that professional football is the quintessential American sport, a magnificent incarnation of our national character. A person can love and admire something while simultaneously feeling major change is needed. That's how many people regard the United States of America, and how we ought to regard its preeminent sport. The NFL does have all kinds of problems. But the game's not over.

# A Not-So-Distant Mirror

The field was a dust bowl as the New York Jets slammed into the Oakland Raiders on a November 1968 day. The Oakland Athletics baseball team had just begun to share Oakland Alameda County Coliseum with the Raiders, and the dirt paths required by baseball made it impossible for groundskeepers to groom good football turf. Problems went beyond swirling dust; the playing surface was 20 feet below sea level, the facility having been constructed with an eccentric sunken-into-the-earth design. The appearance given was that of gladiators in a pit.

The Jets were led by Joe Namath, pro football's glamour boy: touchdown passes, starlets on both arms. Namath's team would go on to defeat the old Baltimore Colts in the Super Bowl that concluded the 1968 season. The Raiders were led by the fearsome Ben Davidson, a six-foot-eight-inch defensive end whose specialty was lifting quarterbacks up and slamming them to the ground. Today that move is a penalty—at the time, the crowd went wild.

The Jets and Raiders were the 1968 season's best teams of the old American Football League, which had not yet been merged into the National Football League. Because they were the best teams, their meeting on this Sunday afternoon was highly anticipated nationally. Oakland and New York had a history of playing nasty, physical games that produced vicious hits and "cart-offs"—injured athletes needing help to the sidelines. That too added to anticipation of the broadcast. And in those simpler, callow days of the NFL, one nationally televised game per week was enough to satisfy fans, so Raiders-Jets was the unquestioned top ticket of the day.

The Raiders' Daryle Lamonica, nicknamed the Mad Bomber for his knack for throwing deep, hit two early touchdown passes as the home team took a 14-6 lead. The Jets rallied, Namath barely eluding Davidson's attempts to dive at his knees. Lamonica hit another touchdown pass, to tie the contest late in the fourth quarter. The Oakland home faithful rose to such a state of intensity it was a wonder they did not sprout fangs and claws. (To a Raiders fan, this is a compliment.) With a minute remaining, the Jets gained a 32-29 lead. Following the kickoff, Lamonica connected with Charlie Smith for a spectacular 78-yard touchdown bomb that appeared to place the hosts in command. But the play was nullified by a yellow flag, and now the Raiders had their backs to the wall. "The team is up against it," as Knute Rockne purportedly said in his perhaps apocryphal 1928 motivational speech about the Gipper.

Tick…tick…tick. Clocks approached 7 p.m. Eastern Time, then the highly regimented start for prime-time programming. Lamonica broke the huddle and brought the Raiders to the line as sound in the Coliseum rose to military-afterburner decibels. Without explanation, the football scene became a vapor. Viewers beheld an adorable mädchen collecting flowers in the Swiss Alps. Readers conversant in football lore know the events being described here as the Heidi Game. NBC cut away from the end of a tense, exciting NFL matchup to the scheduled start of a made-for-television treatment of a children's story.

A network cut away from football! This will not stand!

Pre-Internet, millions of viewers called local radio stations or newspaper sports desks, trying to find out who won. This caused telephone lines to jam in many cities. Pre-cell phone, NBC executives couldn't contact their own control room to instruct that the game be put back on, because telephone trunk lines, overloaded, were producing the screeching old "busy" signal.

When fans learned that seemingly doomed Oakland scored two touchdowns in the final forty-two seconds for a decisive win, there was a sense of national outrage.

Oakland's icing touchdown was recorded by Preston Ridle-huber, not exactly a household name but arguably the most important player in NFL history since, in the wake of the Heidi Game controversy, NBC announced it would always carry every football contest to the conclusion, regardless of the score, field situation or what else might be on the schedule. Other networks promptly matched the policy, which remains in place to this day.

The Heidi Game was pivotal to the evolution of the NFL in many aspects. The lesser aspects had to do with tactics. Both quarterbacks threw for more than 300 yards, with 55 percent of the play calls being passes. Then, such pass-first tactics were seen as revolutionary: eventually, they would become standard. The back-shoulder throw, today spoken of by football announcers as an innovation, was Namath's signature move in the 1960s; the deep fade, also adulated by today's announcers, was Lamonica's favorite throw. Press corners, the stretch draw, tight end seam routes and defensive-line twists, all spoken of today as state-of-the-art, were on display in this 1968 contest.

The larger aspect of the Heidi Game was that it made it official that the United States had become obsessed with professional football. Football wasn't even on TV until 1958; the Cleveland Browns, the best team of the mid-1950s, were fortunate if they performed before forty thousand spectators while others listened in on the radio. Now, the NFL was asserting control over the nation's living rooms. Via the Heidi Game, professional football reached the status of sacrosanct, with huge expansions ahead in ratings, money, numbers of teams and social fascination.

What was the United States like in the year 1968, the year when the NFL embedded itself into American culture?

The United States of 1968 differed from today's nation in fashion, music, hairstyles and fads. What about substantive differences?

In 1968, 40 percent of adults smoked; today, 10 percent do. There were smoking and nonsmoking sections on airplanes, in restaurants and movie theaters. Offices were clouded with tobacco smoke; professional athletes endorsed cigarette brands. Spectators present at the Heidi Game were free to light up, smoking being allowed inside NFL stadia until the early 1990s.

At the time, air pollution was much worse. Since 1968, smog is down 70 percent and acid rain down 80 percent, despite there being far more cars, trucks and buses. Today, cars emit about one-half of 1 percent as much smog-forming chemicals as did cars of the 1960s. A visitor from the present day to 1968 might be struck first by the air—fouled by pollution, thick with tobacco smoke. Compared to 1968, now the air of the United States is a national park at dawn.

When the Heidi Game was played, twenty-three million women worked outside the home; today, sixty-five million do, a huge increase even when factoring for population growth. Then, women were beginning to rival men for bachelor's degrees received. Today, high school girls have higher GPAs and board scores than high school boys, are more likely to enter college and are much more likely to complete their credits and then march in funny robes to Pomp and Circumstance.

In 1968, African Americans faced strong barriers against admission to colleges, to hiring in occupations other than physical labor, and to obtaining housing outside traditional minority neighborhoods. Since then, African American educational and professional achievement has risen steadily, if at a slower pace than hoped.

In 1968, birth outside marriage was rare: 9 percent of American infants were delivered by unwed mothers. Today in the United States, 40 percent of babies arrive either to single mothers or to parents who live together but are not married. Marriage as an institution has declined in concert. In 1968, 72 percent of Americans over the age of twenty-five were married. Today, 49 percent are.

In 1968, same-gender romance was ostracized and, on paper, could be cause for arrest in many states; the Supreme Court did not decriminalize consensual adult gay relations until 2003. By

2015, the Supreme Court had legalized gay marriage, and polls showed wide public support for the concept. The 1968 to 2015 flip-flop—from most heterosexuals married but no gay marriage, to the LGBT community defending marriage more staunchly than heterosexuals—is among the most striking in U.S. social history.

When the Heidi Game was played, Richard Nixon had just been elected president, setting in motion Watergate and the greatest humiliation ever for the American presidency; but also setting in motion the creation of the Environmental Protection Agency, affirmative action programs for African Americans and diplomatic recognition of China.

When the Heidi Game was played, the Vietnam War was raging; the hippie movement was peaking; and the Cold War was at the edge of turning hot. The United States and old Soviet Union in 1968 possessed sixty thousand thermonuclear bombs, enough to end life on Earth. By 2015, America and Russia were down to about 20 percent of that figure, with the arsenals continuing to decline as arms-control treaties become stricter—still awful destructive power but no longer a threat to render the planet lifeless. A visitor from 1968 to the present might be struck first by the clean air, and second by the end of the doomsday threat, two improvements contemporary Americans seem barely aware of.

When the Heidi Game was played, Martin Luther King, Jr. had been recently martyred. The final Civil Rights Act, the one on fair housing, was enacted by Congress a few days after King's April 1968 murder in Memphis. Robert Kennedy recently had been gunned down, ending Camelot in more ways than one.

Powerful demographic shifts were in progress. People were leaving cities for the suburbs in large numbers, though the pattern would reverse by around the year 2000. People were leaving the northeast for the southwest and Florida. Longevity was increasing and rates of nearly all diseases were declining, two patterns that remain today.

A few days after the Heidi Game, the Beatles' *White Album* was released, which turned just a passing fancy. Also a few days after, Yale University announced it would admit women, which turned out to presage fundamental change.

And in the United States of 1968, there were pay phones everywhere. A telephone in your pocket—how absurd is that?

In the present day, America has become a richer, more free, less prejudiced nation with a cleaner environment and better public health; has an ever-worsening inequality problem; has casually run up a national debt that would have shocked even left-wing economists of prior generations; has established some nine hundred military bases in 129 countries;* has elected an African American president; has had African Americans as secretary of state and in consecutive terms running the Department of Justice; and is totally, utterly addicted to professional football.

Few of these turns of events might have been forecast by the world of 1968. From the Heidi Game until our moment, the

---

* Americans tend to shrug at our overseas-based military structure—the sole military in world history that consists entirely of expedition forces intended to fight elsewhere, rather than to defend national borders. Does the United States really need to pay for 174 military bases in Germany? That's the 2015 figure, according to David Vine, a professor at American University.

NFL has assumed an ever-greater role in the life of the nation. When the United States looks into the football mirror, what does it see?

In the structure of football, we see a reflection of America's incredible complexity and power. Thirty-two professional teams, each with fifty-three players, twenty coaches and dozens of other personnel; about five hundred college football teams, each with around a hundred players and ten coaches; about twenty thousand high school teams, each with fifty to a hundred players and five to ten coaches depending on school size. More than ten thousand football games per week in the autumn. Many games played in very large facilities; all games requiring elaborate, expensive equipment.

Only the United States could pull this off! Other nations, even other prosperous nations, are not capable of staging such complex, expensive sporting events in such numbers. America put a man on the moon and built gridiron football culture. No other nation rivals either achievement.

In the football mirror, the United States sees a reflection of its rising affluence. A century ago the sport had followers but was not played at most colleges and high schools because most could not afford football facilities, coaches and equipment. Today, nearly every college and high school fields a football team, many dressed in high-fashion Nike or Under Armour jerseys and wearing the latest concussion-resistant helmets, which cost $250 each. Many colleges and even some high schools now sport alternative jerseys, in keeping with the fashion fad of changing color schemes game by game—an expensive and totally unnecessary novelty. Allen High in Allen, Texas, has a $60 million, eighteen-thousand-seat football stadium with air-conditioned locker rooms and a supersized video scoreboard. More than a hundred universities have NFL-sized football facilities, led by no fewer than eight college football stadia that seat at least a hundred thousand people. Nearly a hundred colleges have both a huge stadium and another full-sized football field dedicated to practice use. A few dozen universities go even further, with both outdoor and indoor full-sized football practice fields, connected to locker rooms that suggest a high-end health club for millionaires. Such football spending may reflect misplaced priorities in education—but the ability to afford the cost shows the nation's increasing prosperity.

The nation's rising affluence is especially pronounced in the NFL reflection. Early on, professional football was performed in open fields or improvised facilities. In 1920, the Akron Pros began their season by defeating the Wheeling Stogies before four thousand paying customers at Akron's League Park, a baseball field with benches for spectators and no showers for players, who arrived at the field already dressed.

Some stadia for professional football were constructed during the Depression by the Works Progress Administration. I grew up in Buffalo, New York, where I watched the Buffalo Bills perform at War Memorial Stadium, a forty-seven-thousand-seat, stonemason-built 1930s facility smack in the center of downtown—there were no parking lots, spectators arriving by bus or streetcar, and seating was austere. Today, the Bills perform in an eighty-thousand-capacity suburban stadium with luxury boxes and private clubs, surrounded by parking lots. That field is modest compared with those of other teams around the league. The Cowboys, 49ers, Giants and Jets play in recently-built stadia that cost more than $1 billion; many other NFL teams boast fields whose total cost, in initial construction plus renovations, is around a billion dollars.

Most of this expense is borne by taxpayers, not the billionaires who own the clubs and keep the profits generated on the subsidized fields—an issue to which this book will return. For now, let us simply marvel at the prosperity reflected in these crown jewels of America's cities. Baltimore, Denver, Houston, Pittsburgh, Seattle and other major U.S. cities today have at their centers gigantic, gleaming facilities for the performance of professional football. Two generations ago, when urban areas were dying, this would have seemed inconceivable.

In football, we also see a reflection of another of America's founding values: teamwork. Americans believe that together we can accomplish more than each could individually. Football, more so than other team sports, is an athletic expression of this viewpoint, but it goes beyond that conceptually as well. Bringing bigger, brighter, more impressive NFL stadia to American cities helped add a sense that teamwork could make cities great places to be. Today, there's so much of this sense that people complain about gentrification not just in Boston and Denver but in Cleveland and Pittsburgh.

Creating urban excitement is a major positive for the NFL. A negative is that professional football holds a mirror up to society's Darwinian economics. Every summer, hundreds of aspiring players are waived by NFL clubs. Most have spent the bulk of their youth and young-adult years preparing for the moment of their NFL tryout, believing riches in the league would be theirs; most were big fish in small ponds at the high school and college levels; most will never earn a dime from playing football, or pick up some token amount as gunners and wedge guys on special teams for a season or two before being waived for a younger player who is willing to sign for less.

Those who do make NFL rosters average $2.4 million per year plus substantial benefits beginning with the fourth season. That the typical NFL career lasts 3.7 years is no coincidence: the fourth season is when players vest for pensions and lifelong health care, so anyone who's not a star is released at the verge of vesting. Nothing or $2.4 million—the kind of dichotomy seen throughout the United States economy. Workers discarded just before they vest for benefits—another standby of the U.S. system.

Perhaps the worst aspect of the American economy is that it's so often winner-take-all. Today, in many occupations, the people at the top roll in money while those below, though little different in ability, struggle to get by. This defect is expressed in the nation's leading sport, and the winnings grow ever-larger. Namath, first selection of the 1965 draft of the old AFL, signed a deal that paid $1.1 million per year*—then, a shocking amount. In summer 2015, quarterback Cam Newton, first selection of the 2011 draft, signed a contract that pays $23 million annually.

In the NFL's mirror, America sees its cult of celebrity. Broadly across our society, a handful of entertainers, politicians and movie stars draw the lion's share of attention, even if only

---

\* All past money figures in this book are converted to 2015 dollars.

slightly more talented than many others who are ignored. The same obtains in the NFL, where quarterbacks such as Peyton Manning or Aaron Rodgers receive more attention than everyone else on their teams combined. In October 2014, when Manning, playing at home, completed a pass that set an NFL record, the Broncos stopped the game so fireworks could fly and their mascot, a gray Arabian named Thunder, could gallop across the field. If any other player on the team had achieved a milestone during the game, Broncos' management would have viewed stopping the game as out of the question. But Manning is a celebrity, and in the NFL as throughout American life, celebrities are treated as aristocracy.

America sees in the NFL mirror its cult of the CEO. Surgeons should earn more than cabdrivers, and CEOs should make more than mailroom personnel. In the contemporary United States, large-company CEOs earn 370 times as much as median workers in their firms: an outrageous level of inequality anchored in the notion that CEOs have godlike importance. This same sense of exaggeration is attached to the NFL's commissioner, Roger Goodell.

Because the NFL is the highest-visibility sport, Goodell has the highest profile of any CEO-like person in athletics: not to mention a $35 million per year salary that is grounded not in market forces but in public subsidies to the NFL. Traveling in police motorcades, waving to the masses as fighter jets execute flyovers above Super Bowls ringed by National Guard members with carbines, Goodell can even seem to have something or other to do with national security. This is smoke-and-mirrors. The NFL's owners hold the real power; Goodell's job is to draw the flack. Essentially, Goodell is a water boy who makes eight figures. But to the extent the NFL holds a mirror to society, he is a reflection of the exaggerated significance contemporary U.S. culture assigns to CEOs.

Goodell's behavior often is a reflection of what U.S. society seems to want from leaders—to see them squirm in public, hear them give lip service to sweeping reform, then go back to business as usual. In 2007, Goodell wrung his hands repeatedly in public over the discovery that the New England Patriots illegally taped opponents' sidelines. Simultaneously Goodell did the Patriots' bidding by destroying the tapes, which came to light only later when it turned out a former team employee retained copies.* When Goodell appeared before the press to discuss the tapes, New England owner Robert Kraft was sitting directly in front of the commissioner, cueing him on what to say and not say. Goodell would squirm in public over the vicious hits bounty scandal at the New Orleans Saints, over deflated footballs in the Patriots-Colts playoff game, over video of Ravens' star Ray Rice punching his fiancée and other matters.

Always it seems Goodell is on the verge of backing some sweeping NFL reform—then the instant society's gaze turns elsewhere, business as usual resumes. Isn't this how oil company CEOs, presidential candidates and others behave? Political leaders often act as though favoring change, then agree behind the scenes to defend the status quo for their constituents.

---

* The former employee with the tapes folded his tent and stole away into the desert immediately after reaching a confidential settlement with the NFL that all but certainly involved a sizeable payment.

Regarding accusations of deflated footballs, Goodell appeared genuinely upset: If something really bad didn't happen, why would the NFL commissioner act to diminish the stature of Tom Brady, one of the sport's meal tickets? Older NFL stars, among them Troy Aikman, expressed disgust for what New England was said to have done. Retired stars want the public to believe NFL achievements come from fair competition, not from games where the fix is in.

Behind the scenes, many of the thirty-one bosses who do not own the New England Patriots were pressuring Goodell to slap the Flying Elvii down.* Under Bill Belichick, the Patriots have made a spectacular six Super Bowl appearances in fifteen seasons, while missing the postseason only thrice: year in, year out, Belichick takes unknown players other teams have discarded and molds them into efficient winners. A number of NFL owners have long felt this could only happen if the Patriots were cheating. Other owners were furious when New England was caught in 2007 using video cameras to cheat; a fair number of them felt the punishment meted out to the Patriots was too light. When another Patriots cheating scandal began in 2015, other owners wanted to lower the boom this time.

So Goodell appeased the anti-New England owners by being really mean to Brady in public, even if this reduced the dazzle power of one of football's most marketable stars, while also appeasing Kraft by not vacating the Super Bowl win, as the NCAA has annulled football victories tainted by improper be-

---

* The Patriots' helmet logo looks like a flying Elvis; I contend that "Elvii" is the proper plural of Elvis.

havior. This reflects what America seems to like in leaders—showy PR combined with studious avoidance of substance.

Another reflection the NFL produces has to do with masculinity. Increasingly, the media elite look down on manhood, depicting male behavior and male impulses as things to be ashamed of—Bruce Jenner becoming Caitlyn Jenner was such a huge media hit in part because Jenner symbolically rejected his manhood. Contemporary academia intensely detests all aspects of maleness. More broadly across society, men are being devalued economically, are presumed guilty until proven innocent by new campus conduct codes, often are absent from the home owing to their own irresponsibility or are confined in prison owing to America's methodical locking up of young males.

Turnabout is fair play: perhaps the current low standing of manhood in American society is karmic retribution for centuries of male bias against women. But no society can reject masculinity altogether. Here the NFL enters the picture, providing a source of masculine images—a place where manhood can be celebrated while carefully walled off from the rest of society.

The players are strong and fearless, true manly-men. Except in a few disturbing cases, players are polite, clean-shaven role models who do volunteer work and call everyone "sir" or "ma'am." What kid wouldn't want an NFL player for a big brother! Football stars are imaginary big brothers to large numbers of American tweens, while football coaches are father-figures to a society that longs for actual fathers.

In the NFL mirror, the nation sees its ongoing racial story. For society as a whole, many indicators are positive—African

Americans in high government positions, rising black house-hold income and education levels, overt racism diminished. But many negatives continue, including police mistreatment of blacks and low reading and math levels in many mostly-black schools.

When the nation looks into the NFL mirror, it beholds African American males earning substantial incomes while serving as heroic figures to the mass audience. Whites all over the country cheer for black NFL stars, holding them up to their children as persons to be emulated. That's a clear positive. The nation also sees a league with 70 percent African American players compared to 15 percent African American head coaches, 10 percent African American general managers, and no African American owners. When it comes to muscle-power roles, professional football is completely merit-based and post-racial: management and economic power is different. All one need do to visualize the genuine-but-halting character of U.S. racial progress is to inspect an NFL sideline.

There is a final, larger way in which the NFL holds up a mirror to the American experiment.

With the end of World War II, the United States became the strongest country in the world—and began paying more attention to a sport that celebrates strength.

Football popularity made its first big leap in the decade after the war. Perhaps the principal reason was the tremendous expansion of the public university system, made possible by G.I. Bill tuition funding and rising prosperity that increased state university budgets. The latter expanded love of football from the small private colleges that initially dominated the game—

under Teddy Roosevelt, Princeton, Harvard, Yale, Swarthmore and the University of Chicago were the football powers—to the much larger state-university landscape.

Attendance at college and NFL contests took off in the 1950s, the same time America was emerging as the strongest nation ever. Early in the 1990s, the popularity of the NFL made another leap, judged in every way—higher ratings, more spectators, much higher television-rights fees, millions wearing NFL-branded apparel, a corporate rush to affiliate with pro football for advertising purposes.

One reason for the second big popularity jump was that the league and its union achieved labor peace; there hasn't been an NFL strike since 1987, assuring the supply of high-quality competition. But what else happened in the early 1990s? The Cold War ended. At that juncture the United States emerged as not just the strongest nation of the moment but the strongest ever in the history of the world—arguably, a single country more powerful than all others combined.

And as America became the most muscular nation the world has known, it bestowed more attention on the most muscular of sports, football.

From the beginning of the postwar era to the present day, American strength and wealth have steadily risen while American enthusiasm for gridiron football increased in lockstep. Throughout this period, one of the seminal questions facing the United States body politic has been: What is the proper use of power?

In the Koreas, Vietnam, the Persian Gulf, Afghanistan, Libya, the Philippines, Panama, El Salvador, Nicaragua, Iraq and elsewhere, America's leaders, soldiers and citizens have wrestled with the ethical quandaries of how to exert power within a structure of rules. The quandaries continue as the sole-great-power status of the United States continues.

When we watch the NFL, the most muscular of sports, we are watching a game in which the players wrestle with the proper exercise of their strength. The NFL is an athletic interpretation of a core issue facing the United States: how to use incredible power with self-restraint.

A superpower with mixed emotions about its own might: that is the contemporary United States. That's what we see in the NFL mirror. And that is why we can't look away.

# What Comedians Know About Football

The inaugural episode of *Saturday Night Live* aired in October 1975, and the subject of the very first monologue was football. Comedian George Carlin set out to laud baseball, then beginning to lose its status as America's pastime, and denounce the usurper, which he found quasi-military. Or, in Carlin's words, "Football is a ground acquisition game. You knock the crap out of eleven guys and take their land away from them."

Carlin went on to offer this comparison:

"In football, the object is for the quarterback, also known as the field general, to be on target with his aerial assault, riddling the defense by hitting his receivers with deadly accuracy in spite of the blitz, even if he has to use a shotgun. With short bullet passes and long bombs, he marches his troops into enemy territory, balancing this aerial assault with a sustained ground attack that punches holes in the forward wall of the enemy's defensive line. In baseball, the object is to go home—and to be safe!"*

---

* In his *SNL* appearance, Carlin stumbled several times under the pressure of live national TV. I've quoted improved wording he later devised for his standup act.

THE GAME'S NOT OVER

Perhaps because Carlin, who died in 2008, always presented himself as a hippie—he wore long hair in a period before it was common to encounter men with ponytails at corporate business meetings—one might assume his scolding of football was the counterculture speaking. But today, the comedian's perceptions ring just as true as they did a generation ago. His statement, "Baseball is a nineteenth-century pastoral game, football is a twentieth-century technological struggle" hits the nail on the head.

Performing his routine in 1975, Carlin saw the martial aspect of football as essential to understanding the moment. The Vietnam War had just concluded, the military was losing standing in American society. Simultaneously the role of armed forces in a free society was undergoing a fundamental shift. In past generations, acceptance of a stint in the military was nearly universal, beyond those such as Mennonites who were true pacifists: men either actively wanted to serve or grudgingly agreed that they must. By the Vietnam period, resistance to induction had become common. Congress decided to end the draft, the final year for mandatory conscription in the United States being 1973. The all-volunteer service that replaced conscription entailed higher pay and better treatment for soldiers and sailors, but also tended to make the military into a separate world with which many Americans had scant connections. Adjusting for population growth, an American was three times as likely to serve in the military during the Vietnam War as to serve today.

As the military role in American communities began to shrink in the 1970s, ever more enthusiasm was transferred to football, a sort of war-lite. Young men who in earlier genera-tions would have gone to boot camp instead were going to training camp. Football has uniforms and intense discipline like the military, has organized units marching to seize territory like the military, has tight chains of command like the military—but no guns and no morally fraught intervention in the affairs of other nations. As the United States grew cool to its armed forces, many emotions associated with real war were transferred to a war-lite sport.

While pundits think about the military in terms of foreign policy and global power projection, for much of America, armed forces appreciation is a pivotal element of small-town life: cause for parades and other community events, something nearly ev-eryone had a family member involved in. Military awareness is important for cities, too. Many show keen civic mindfulness of armed forces service by their citizens, often constructing mon-uments, such as Memorial Park in Houston and the Garden of Remembrance in Seattle.

The miasma of Vietnam, closely followed by the end of widespread service via conscription, changed this. Communities needed a new focal point—something entire towns or cities could rally around.

There are communities where baseball, basketball or ice hockey are the hub of civic pride, but football fills this role bet-ter than other sports. Football is the most complicated of ath-letic events, requiring the most participants both in pads and behind the scenes; and draws the largest crowds. For every one player who goes on the field, there are three or four other people who had a role in making the game possible. That means, just as once large numbers of American families had a member with military service, large numbers of American families would have a member with involvement in football—and it was something the family could beam with pride about without engaging the moral ambiguities of Vietnam, or, today, Iraq.

The positive aspect of football as a community rallying point is poorly understood by the nation's media leaders, for a simple reason—they're nearly all in New York City, where many public schools and private prep schools can't offer football, owing to space constraints. And from Manhattan, it's a hike to the nearest university that emphasizes football.* The result is that the nation's news-media elite, which never had much connection to military culture, today has little connection to what came next, football culture.

That their own kids generally don't participate in football may cause Manhattan opinion-makers to view the gridiron sport as something for rubes in the sticks. When the Super Bowl was played in the Big Apple in 2014—bearing in mind that for NFL purposes, New York City is located in New Jersey—the *New York Times* and the *New Yorker* responded with a collective shrug, barely seeming to acknowledge the contest. "Super Bowl—that's all it is, just the Super Bowl?" may be the sort of thing a jaded New Yorker would say. But lack of personal familiarity with the upside of football sociology, especially its

---

* With the Giants and Jets decamped to New Jersey and Columbia University football in a decades-long slump, the Fordham University Rams, performing at Coffey Field in the Bronx, in recent years have been the most-fun football accessible via the New York City subway. The Rams play an entertaining uptempo style, and Fordham has high admission standards for athletics.

community-spirit value, causes one of the instances of disso-
nance between the media stratosphere and average Americans.

As everywhere outside New York City, more civic attention
turned to the sport, the National Football League, its highest
level, grew in status. Football evoked some of the positives associated with forming armies—personal courage, demonstrations of might, the community pulling together—without any
of the negatives. Handsome young men went into something
akin to battle, using their bodies fearlessly, returning nicely
bloodied but not really harmed. (Realization that there could be
hidden neurological damage would come later.) Coaches barked
orders like officers, and were treated with ceremonial deference.
Baseball players may address their managers by first name.
Football coaches, even to millionaire NFL stars, invariably are
"sir." It wasn't just the lexicon of "blitz," "bomb," and "ram it
down their throats." The terminology which made for an amus-
ing Carlin comedy routine was largely coincidence. But the
symbolism was not. To a nation drained by Vietnam and unset-
tled by the pall it cast over militarism, football was welcome as
offering the same authority structure without the life-or-death
consequences.

More indication of George Carlin's insight: he was right on
the money by using television to offer his critique of football.
The tube was at that moment beginning a burst of growth. A
new idea, transmission via cable, had come about with the 1972
founding of Home Box Office.* ESPN would launch in 1979,

---

* Today, this company is just HBO, the way KFC no longer stands for
Kentucky Fried Chicken and TCU, not Texas Christian University, is now
the name of the college.

CNN in 1980. Soon the range of programming available to a house or apartment would increase exponentially. A lot of that programming would be sports, an endlessly renewable resource; and a lot of the sports programming would be football.

Thus as Carlin walked onto the stage at 30 Rock, two major social transitions—decline of the military as an aspect of daily life and expansion of television—favored a bigger role for the NFL. A third major factor, that the game itself was becoming more exciting, will be the subject of the next chapter.

For further insights into the expansion of the NFL, let's turn to another comedian, Adam Carolla, cohost of the Comedy Central hit *The Man Show*. In the 1999 pilot, Carolla warned his presumptively male audience, "In 50 years, we'll all be chicks." Women, Carolla said on the show and in standup routines, were taking over and resistance was futile. All men could hope for was to drink beer, ogle bikini models and watch football. Otherwise, the cause was lost.

Consider what was happening to women, and to women's issues, as NFL popularity accelerated. The steep increase in women working outside the home was accompanied by a lowering of the barriers to women in many arenas of society. The Civil Rights Act of 1964—the one that followed the assassination of John F. Kennedy, and after a two-month Southern filibuster, passed the Senate in tribute to him—mainly banned discrimination on the basis of race, but also prohibited hiring discrimination on the basis of gender. On the day of passage of the act, there were few women in positions of power in government and business. Now there have been several female secretaries of state; a female Speaker of the House; female CEOs not just at consumer products companies but at heavy-manufacturing firms including Lockheed Martin, the world's largest defense contractor.

The rise of power for women was as it should be, but for many men created a sense of unease. Places that were once male preserves—the president's cabinet, the corporate boardroom, the faculty club—were trending toward double-X. Girls and women were no longer playing just the "skirt sports" (tennis and field hockey), but basketball, soccer and lacrosse.

Women might take over the Justice Department and defense contractors; surely a female president is in the cards. But there was one place women could never, ever rule—football. Women could be play-by-play announcers: Beth Mowins calls a football game as well as any man. They might be officials: in 2015, Sarah Thomas became the NFL's first female zebra. Women might be athletic trainers and may someday be NFL coaches: Jen Welter was a coaching intern, an entry-level position, at the 2015 Arizona Cardinals summer camp.[*] But there was no way a woman could suit up in the NFL. In fifty years, the players will not be chicks.

Technically, the NFL is open to both genders. League spokesman Greg Aiello said in 2006, "The NFL has no male-

---

[*] Welter coached inside linebackers, telling them when to crash, when to drop and when to string out. These days you just don't run into that many women who say, "I coach linebackers." But a generation from now, dorm-room dialogue may go like this:

College guy #1: So who'd you meet at the party?

College guy #2: This girl who's the new offensive coordinator. She was hot. She gave me her prefrontal cortex routing code.

College guy #1: Nice! But seems like you always meet football coaches. When are you going to meet some girl who's an art history major?

only rule. All human beings are eligible, as long as they are three years out of high school and have a usable football skill set." Only human beings eligible—there will never be a Klingon cornerback! A few girls have played varsity football in high school, and at least two women have been placekickers for NCAA teams. But the physical requirements of the NFL—the mass and muscle—are so rare in women that a female player seems all but impossible.

Life is full of unintended consequences: rising power and freedom for women had the unintended consequence of encouraging men to be more enthusiastic about football, a social sector where women could never take over. In turn, women who liked football became able to watch and root unapologetically, no longer having to make tomboy jokes to justify their interest. It was a nice conjunction for the NFL.

Women do play one high-profile part in professional football, that of leading cheers. This fit the male-retreat view of the game: the only role for women was to look pretty and praise the men.

In an obvious way, it's ridiculous that NFL team Web sites now offer softcore porn. Annually, the Philadelphia Eagles cheerleaders pose in lingerie, and clicking on the cheerleaders button of the Eagles' Web site leads to a warning page that announces, "Please note, this area contains mature content." But by bringing a hint of the risqué into mainstream entertainment, the NFL's sideline women not only help sell the product, they represent another reflection of society in the mirror. During the 1960s, there was tremendous tension between erotic experimentation and traditional monogamy. The middle ground that evolved was that most Americans did not want to be viewed as prudes, but also did not approve of libertinism. A kind of corporate-endorsed look-but-don't-touch sexual ideal emerged, and NFL cheerleaders are its exemplars.*

The NFL's bombshell cheerleaders sure played well on television. It would turn out everything about football played well on television.

Before cable arrived in the late 1970s and early 1980s, the typical TV set received the three legacy networks, a PBS channel, and perhaps a regional "superstation" airing old movies. Soon channels were proliferating, bringing with them the need to fill airtime. The NFL would increase in stages from two broadcast games per week shown in most cities in the 1970s to six today. In 1984, the Supreme Court deregulated the broadcasting of college football, upping NCAA play from one nationally televised game per week to, today, about twenty-five college football games weekly for basic-cable viewers, and around forty-five college games per week for those who opt for a sports-tier package.† Today, NFL games air nationally on Sunday, Monday, Thursday and some Saturdays: big-college

---

* That cheerleaders show skin isn't exploitation—the scantily clad dancing girl has a long history in entertainment. The exploitation is financial. Most NFL teams pay the cheerleaders token sums, typically $100 per game and nothing to rehearse. Roger Goodell is paid $170,000 per hour. When rehearsal and corporate-marketing appearances are included, most NFL cheerleaders make about $2 an hour.

† In the 1980s, the NCAA tried to restrict telecasts as part of a power struggle with the College Football Association, then the marketing arm of major conferences. Freed by the Supreme Court of the need for NCAA approval, the conferences soon realized they didn't need the College Football Association either—a Supreme Court victory set in motion its demise.

football contests dominate the airwaves on Thursdays, Fridays and Saturdays. Networks have dipped their toes into Tuesday and Wednesday prime-time football telecasts. An ultimate NFL—a Nonstop Football League—may someday happen.

Football and television potentiated each other because football is a stop-action sport. Downs are over in a few seconds, leaving time in between snaps for an instant replay that helps viewers understand what occurred. Basketball, ice hockey and soccer are continuous action, while baseball consists almost entirely of stoppage: none are just-so for the production format of TV. Football offers the right mix of something happening, then play immediately stopping so what occurred can be reviewed and analyzed. Football seemingly was invented for the instant replay.

Because pro football teams play only sixteen regular season contests—Major League Baseball teams jog onto the diamond 162 times per year, National Basketball Association teams tip off eighty-two times—each NFL game offers a sense of importance and electricity missing from other sports. Television wants to create the feeling that what's being aired is not merely interesting but exciting. Football was not designed with television in mind, but seemed as if it were.

As the universe of cable expanded infinitely, just like the real universe, legacy-network prime-time ratings began to erode. Playback devices such as VCRs and DVRs, then the posting of TV serials on the Web, reduced the share of viewers who watched an initial airing. Once, hit TV shows were like the nation's campfire—much of the country gathered at the same moment to view the final episode of *M*A*S*H*. As on-demand viewing threw a bucket of water on the campfire aspect of TV shows, one type of programming still got everyone on the couch watching at the same moment, live sports. And pro football is the best drawing card of live sports.

Networks began to realize the NFL was the anchor store of the television mall—what lured viewers in the door.

*Monday Night Football* began in 1970, on ABC. Then, the American Broadcasting Company was seen as the junior varsity network, a poor third behind golden-age networks CBS (home of Walter Cronkite) and NBC (whose 1955 live telecast of *Peter Pan* was TV's first holy-cow moment). Landing an NFL contract, and placing the games in prime time, elevated ABC to equal status with CBS and NBC.

*Sunday Night Football* began on ESPN in 1987. Then, ESPN was a quirky niche product for sports nuts. In the 1980s, it was not clear the whole country would go cable—after all, why pay for what you can get free using rabbit-ear antennas? The NFL's move to the new transmission technology was central to the 95 percent market penetration cable would achieve by the year 2000: Comcast and Time-Warner would not be what they are today if pro football hadn't embraced wiring up homes. As had happened with ABC and *Monday Night Football*, the *Sunday Night Football* decision put ESPN on the national map. Today, the Bristol, Connecticut-based firm—its headquarters looks like a CIA installation, grim buildings and arrays of gigantic dishes pointed toward satellites—operates seven channels and continues to hoover up sports broadcast rights.

When Fox—initially styled as the Fox Broadcasting Company, to resemble its older brothers—debuted in 1985, the public was unimpressed. Fox's stated goal of joining the big three as the fourth primary network seemed quixotic. In 1993, Fox wrestled away from CBS a share of NFL rights, knocking the Tiffany Network out of pro football broadcasting. This legitimized Fox, whose news, drama and comedy programming today owe their existence to the NFL.

CBS would fight to get back into the NFL business, winning a rights deal in 1997. During the interregnum, Sunday afternoon ratings for CBS were bleak, further convincing network executives that professional football was a must-have. Now all networks nervously await the next round of NFL negotiations, fearing that failure to secure some pro football contract would knock a broadcasting company to subordinate status. This is one of the many kinds of leverage the NFL possesses over television, leading to ever-more-lofty rights fees.

In 2015, the NFL signed a live-streaming deal with Yahoo. Always a Web search leader, Yahoo had been struggling to reinvent itself as a media conglomerate, and was taking it on the chin on Wall Street. Will the NFL's imprimatur—association with its American-flag-like "shield"*—do for that company what it did for ABC, ESPN and Fox?

In the contemporary arrangement, NFL television rights have something in common with defense contracts—spread around to create a broad base of lobbying support. Professional football has image-broadcast agreements with AT&T (owner of DirecTV), CBS, Comcast (owner of NBC), Disney (owner

---

* The NBA logo is a silhouette of Jerry West driving up the court, the MLB logo is a slugger about to swing at a pitch. The NFL logo is red-white-and-blue, including white stars on a blue background.

of ABC and most of ESPN), Fox, Hearst (owner of the rest of ESPN), NBC, Verizon and Yahoo. This puts the league's fantastic entertainment products practically everywhere—and also gives a sizeable share of the Fortune 500 a financial stake in NFL subsidies and in not criticizing the NFL's downsides, a subject we'll return to.

For now, what matters is that television and professional football have been sweethearts since they first laid eyes on each other, and the romance continues.

Given that football is wedded to television, we may as well learn to watch it better. All NFL partner networks do a fine job with camera angles, replays and other aspects of cinematography. If you're attending an NFL contest, go early and wander behind the stadium, where the network trucks park. You'll behold a D-Day-like deployment of equipment—dozens of vehicles up on jacks to keep them level when the stadium shakes, entire portable control rooms, generator trucks for the extra wattage required, antennas pointed to the heavens.

The equipment brought along by television networks is always impressive; the announcers brought along by television networks may be another matter. Television football announcers may seem barely to be watching what's happening on the field. They're chortling about some celebrity they met in pregame warmups, or obsessing over views of the owner's box. Television constantly shows views of the owners as part of the general sucking-up to the league powers that be—Dan Snyder, owner of the Washington franchise, does not like to be shown, a source of ongoing confusion with camera crews.

Sometimes TV football announcers express confusion about

things that would be obvious to anyone paying attention. That's because the announcers aren't looking at the field, they are looking at the little tetragon of the TV image on the monitors in front of them, while spotters whisper into their earpieces. Because the TV tetragon focuses on the quarterback, TV announcers spotlight the quarterback. But 90 percent of football happens away from the ball. On television, it's quarterback quarterback quarterback; then a view of the owner's box; then a reference to some airheaded celebrity; then a view of the head coach. From the latter we learn that coaches look happy after a good play and after a bad play, grimace.

Listen to any good radio announcer and you'll hear what the wide receivers are doing, what coverages the defense is in, who on the line is playing well and who isn't. Radio play-by-play types almost uniformly call games better than television announcers. The radio play-by-play person has to paint a picture with words—and so must pay close attention to the action. Radio play-by-play people do their own homework rather than rely on fact sheets handed them by flunkies, making the radio announcers knowledgeable. Nine times out of ten, the radio call of an NFL broadcast will be superior to the television call.*

In a moment, I will offer suggestions about where to look when at the game and how to handle the remote when watch-

---

* Top NFL flagship radio talent includes Paul Allen (Minnesota Vikings), Wes Durham (Atlanta Falcons), Bob Lamey (Indianapolis Colts), Wayne Larrivee (Green Bay Packers), Dave Logan (Denver Broncos), John Murphy (Buffalo Bills), Greg Papa (Oakland Raiders), Steve Raible (Seattle Seahawks) and Merrill Reese (Philadelphia Eagles).

ing from the couch. First, the worst thing about television announcers—their platitudes:

*"He's wide open!"* Often this is said of a receiver who is tackled as he catches the ball. In prep play, receivers may be wide open. At the NFL level, this almost never happens—the receiver is open if there's enough separation for the passer to zing the ball just past the defender's reach.

*"This is a bad time for a penalty!"* When is a good time?

*"They're giving 110 percent!"* No they're not.

*"It's a blitz!"* Television extols the blitz because this tactic produces big plays—though as often for the offense as for the defense.[*] Announcers tend to cry "blitz!" whenever a linebacker moves toward the quarterback. But it's only a blitz if at least five men rush.[†]

*"He's really got athleticism!"* Sounds like an incurable disease.

*"It's a double reverse!"* Probably it's not even a reverse.

Most of the plays TV announcers call a "reverse" actually are the end-around: quarterback hands to an outside guy who's running laterally. The ball has never reversed, that is, never started toward one edge of the field, then changed direction.

Most plays that TV announcers call a "double reverse" actually

---

[*] TV announcers like the blitz more than do NFL defensive coordinators. The last four Super Bowl winners—New England, Seattle, Baltimore, and the New York Giants—rarely blitzed in their title seasons.

[†] In the zone-rush scheme pioneered by the Pittsburgh Steelers, and now employed by about half the NFL's clubs, before the snap five to seven men appear to be about to blitz. At the snap four actually rush, while the others drop off. Because one of the players who rushes is a linebacker, announcers tend to cry, "It's a blitz!" though four, the standard number of pass rushers, have crossed the line.

are a single reverse—Runner A starts in one direction, Runner B takes the ball going the opposite way. Double reverses are rare because they involve Runner A going one way, then Runner B going the other way, then Runner C going back in the original direction. The Cowboys once attempted a double reverse in the Super Bowl and never got to the Runner C stage, losing 9 yards.

A triple reverse would be nearly impossible to execute: Runner A going one way, then Runner B going the other way, then Runner C going in the original direction, then Runner D headed back in Runner B's direction. I have watched an enormous amount of football at the high school, college and pro levels and never witnessed a triple reverse. Should you ever hear a TV announcer cry, "It's a triple reverse!" rest assured it was not.

*"If he hadn't [been tackled/fallen down/dropped the pass/tripped over his own teammate], he could have gone all the way!"* A subset of this announcer platitude is,

*"It was almost intercepted!"* Interceptions are more exciting than routine downs, so TV announcers root for them. When a lunging defender comes near a pass, TV announcers may declare, "It was almost intercepted!" But plays described as "almost intercepted!" usually are not. Defenders are less likely than receivers to catch passes in the first place.[*] Often what's said to be "almost intercepted!" was a pass that a defender barely tipped with an outstretched hand. Of course, if it had been intercepted and he hadn't been tackled, he could have gone all the way!

---

[*] The receiver knows where the ball will go, the defender does not. The receiver usually is moving away from the ball while the defender usually is moving toward the pass, which means it hits the defender's hands harder than it hits the receiver's hands.

*"Unbelievable!"* Television announcers are not satisfied that plays be exciting, they must be "unbelievable!" You just saw it with your own eyes—why don't you believe it?

The above comments are sufficiently generic, they don't require attribution. Here are my all-time favorite inane TV football announcer remarks, by speaker:

Phil Simms of CBS: "Tony Romo is a great quarterback who played a great, great game." Said of Romo after he threw three interceptions in a home loss.[*]

Rich Gannon of CBS: "The San Francisco offense is getting too predictable. The 49ers are either running or passing."

Tony Siragusa of Fox, speaking of a play by Eli Manning: "He did a fantastic job of using his eyes to look at the defense."

Now, two tips. They work for me, and may work for you:

When attending a game, don't look at the offense before the snap—look at how the defense lines up. This is an aspect of football that can't be observed in the ball-focused tetragon of the TV. How many defenders are deep and how many are pressing the line of scrimmage? As the quarterback begins his cadence, locate and count the safeties. You'll be doing exactly what the quarterback is doing at that instant. Soon what happens after the snap will make a lot more sense to you.

When watching at home, turn the sound off on your television.[†]

---

[*] Simms and Jon Gruden of ESPN are among happy-talk TV announcers who depict everyone as above average. If Simms saw a yak herder leading bovidae across the steppe, Simms might say, "He's a great, great yak herder and the yaks are really buying into his program."

[†] Some turn off the TV announcers and listen to the play-by-play radio call. The five-second discord between TV and radio signals limits the practicality of this workaround.

Eliminating the numbing patter, laff-track chortles and celebrity tie-in plugs will elevate your senses to the contest itself. Watch a few football games with the announcers turned off. You'll be amazed at how your appreciation of the sport improves.

And if you have a surround-sound or home-entertainment system, there's a way to mute the booth crew yet hear crowd reactions—in other words, to experience at home what you would in the stands. Google "5.1 turn off announcers" for instructions on hearing the crowd but not the patter.

The march of the NFL into our homes has made professional football inseparable from the country's perception of itself. Of course, some people have no interest in sports, but it may be safe to say that large numbers of American home viewers watch ten hours of football for every one hour of news or cultural programming. Perhaps the next stage in communication technology will offer ways for viewers to enjoy pro football's terrific athletic quality without the corporate hoo-ha. For now, we should be more discerning consumers, and the first step is to turn the announcers off.

IIIIIIIIIIIIIIIIIIIIIIIIIIIIIII ③ IIIIIIIIIIIIIIIIIIIIIIIIIIIIIII

# How the NFL Got Game

In January 1978, the Dallas Cowboys faced the Denver Broncos in the Super Bowl at New Orleans. Players were visibly lighter than today's, and lacking the tree-trunk biceps on display in the contemporary NFL. Cowboys' starting left tackle Ralph Neely was considered a giant at 265 pounds: today, Neely would be undersized at any major college program. Both teams operated exclusively from the huddle, with quarterbacks under center. The no-huddle offense and the shotgun formation, now viewed as keys to success, then were considered desperation tactics for losers. Dallas coach Tom Landry wore a sport coat, tie and fedora, his Denver counterpart Red Miller trotted out in khakis and a golf shirt—another decade would pass before it occurred to anyone to dress NFL coaches in branded apparel for marketing purposes. Halftime entertainment featured the drill team from a nearby junior college.

Differences in atmospherics aside, the contest seemed a candidate for sports lore. The Broncos and Cowboys had the league's best regular season records that year, so the Super Bowl pairing was ideal. Dallas fielded four players, plus a coach, who later would don the garish yellow blazer of the Pro Football

Hall of Fame in Canton, Ohio—Tony Dorsett, Landry, Roger Staubach, Randy White and Rayfield Wright. Denver responded with stars Lyle Alzado, Randy Gradishar, Tom Jackson and Haven Moses, and with quarterback Craig Morton, who'd already won a Super Bowl. Both teams had catchy nicknames: the Broncos were the Orange Crush, the Cowboys replied with the Doomsday Defense. The table appeared set for a monster contest.

Instead, the game was a yawner. Dallas led 13-0 after a plodding first half. With the Cowboys ahead 20-10 in the fourth quarter, the Broncos' Miller ordered his charges to punt inside Dallas territory, a timorous decision the football gods promptly punished with a 27-10 Dallas victory. The Dallas defense held Denver to just 35 yards passing, a harrowing number even considering Morton left the game injured and was replaced by the legendary Norris Weese.

In team sports there is perennial debate regarding whether a low score and weak stats means poor offense or good defense. This question, which cannot be resolved, is a pleasant topic for debate over craft-brewed ale. But the dullsville 1978 Super Bowl followed other low-scoring, yawn-inspiring final contests, including Pittsburgh's 16-6 win over Minnesota a few years before. For followers of the winning team, a stellar day on defense is exciting. The national television audience by and large does not find stalled drives captivating.

A short time after the 1978 Super Bowl, the NFL's rules committee made a seemingly minor change. Till then, defensive backs had been allowed to contact receivers anywhere on the field and as often as they wanted, until the pass was released:

wide receiver and cornerback could engage in an extended shoving match as they headed up the field. Defensive coordinators called this tactic "bump-and-run." Big, strong corner Lem Barney of the Detroit Lions was the master of bump-and-run. He'd hammer receivers again and again as they tried to get downfield. If you were a Lions' fan, the result was fantastic, as was Barney's eventual receipt of a garish blazer at Canton. For everyone else, the result was dull.

So, in 1978, the NFL instituted a "chuck" zone. Within 5 yards of the line of scrimmage, a defender could hit—chuck—a receiver once. Just once, and as soon as the receiver was 5 yards downfield, further deliberate contact would draw a flag. Purists were outraged. Barney responded by retiring, sensing no place for him in the new order.

About those purists—they were outraged by the 24-second clock in basketball, the designated hitter rule in baseball and the helmet in ice hockey. In football, purists once were outraged by the forward pass, by the grabbing the face mask penalty (until 1962, an NFL defender legally could tackle the ballcarrier by his face mask), and by banning of the clothesline (slamming one's arm into an opponent's neck). Sports rules fundamentally are arbitrary. The tablets Moses received on Mount Sinai did not specify that a field goal counts for 3 points (at various times in the NFL's past, field goals counted for 5 or 4 points) or that a pass can come from anywhere behind the line of scrimmage (until 1933, the quarterback had to be at least 5 yards back). Arbitrary sports rules can be changed when the spirit moves, and most rules changes have made sports more interesting, less dangerous, or both.

First imposed in 1978, the chuck rule would be made stricter in 1996, and then became an officiating "point of emphasis" in 2004—these words being a warning to players that zebras were watching for a particular foul. The new standards began a transformation in professional football tactics, opening up the passing game.

Other rule changes were in the cards. Morton left the Super Bowl feeling dizzy following a body-slam sack.[*] Concussion was then a taboo word—real men didn't care how much their heads hurt! But owners have tremendous economic investments in NFL quarterbacks, and don't want to see their capital writhing on the ground. Fans have an interest in quarterbacks not being injured, too: good teams may promptly go downhill, ruining a season. For instance, in 2014, the Arizona Cardinals opened 9-1 and had the inside track to become the first NFL club to host the Super Bowl in its own stadium. Then injuries ended the years of Arizona's first- and second-string quarterbacks, the Cardinals closing 2-5 with several dreadful performances.

So another rule change of 1978 liberalized use of hands by offensive linemen, in order to make it harder for pass rushers to reach the quarterback. The head-slap move was also banned. Previously, a pass rusher could punch his gloved hand against the helmet of a blocker, causing the opponents' ears to ring.

Lots of head slaps sounded like a formula for cumulative neurological damage to linemen, but it wasn't anonymous offensive linemen with whom rules committees were concerned. Banning the head-slap improved protection of the quarterback.

---

[*] In 2013, Morton joined a lawsuit against the NFL, alleging his concussion was improperly treated.

In 1977, the season before the head-slap was prohibited and offensive linemen were granted more leeway to block, 8.9 percent of NFL dropbacks resulted in a sack. By 2014, the sack share was down to 6.3 percent, even though pass-first offenses meant defensive ends could lock in on the quarterback, not worrying about the run.*

Rules changes to favor passing offense continued. In 2006, it would become illegal to dive at the quarterback's legs, an old ploy to knock the other side's signal-caller out of the game. In 2009, a defender was no longer allowed to launch himself into a receiver after the pass had gone by, an old ploy to intimidate receivers by hammering them when they were in a defenseless posture.† In 2012, contact with the quarterback's helmet and neck was prohibited, unless the quarterback left the pocket and became a running back. In 2012 came the most important rule change for safety since the banning of grabbing the face mask: deliberate helmet-to-helmet hits were prohibited.‡

---

* Television announcers tend to say that defensive ends who know the offense is about to pass can "pin their ears back." In order to what, decrease their aerodynamic coefficient of drag? Horses are able to pin their ears back; Homo sapiens cannot. "Pin their ears back" is the sort of phrase people use though having no idea what it means, like "raining cats and dogs."

† This is the "defenseless receiver" rule, defenseless in this sense meaning the receiver is reaching for the pass and unable to protect himself from a defender he cannot see. In 2011 and 2013, the NFL would extend the definition of "defenseless" to any player who cannot see a hit coming, except in the chaotic tackle box, the zone where the linemen face off. There, it's still pretty much anything goes.

‡ The National Federation of High Schools banned the deliberate helmet-to-helmet hit in 2009, and the NCAA banned the tactic in 2010. This is one of many instances in which the NFL has lagged behind safety reforms at other levels of the sport, rather than being a leader institution.

THE GAME'S NOT OVER

Though this new protection extended to all players, in effect it was another favor to the offense, since the most common category of deliberate helmet-to-helmet impact was safeties hammering receivers.

The arc of offense-first rules changes was denounced by Hall of Famer Jerry Rice[*] as heralding an era of "powder-puff football." Yet if traditionalists had succeeded in preventing the forward pass from becoming legal—lofting a pass is not manly, not like bloody noses in the trenches!—Rice's own career never would have happened.

Rice was not alone; many retired stars objected to NFL rule changes intended to make the game less risky. Those who performed under the old rules and lived to tell the tale seemed to want credit for being so ultra-macho that they laughed at vicious hits. Indeed, the "brush" gesture—after sustaining a knockout hit, jumping up and brushing imaginary dirt off one's jersey, to show contempt for danger—was a testimony to machismo. But the new rules did not just reduce vicious hits, though that would have been justification enough. The new rules increased scoring, which made games more entertaining.

In 1977, the final season before the chuck rule, on average, NFL teams combined to score 34.2 points per game. That number would rise in nearly linear fashion to 41.4 points per game at the turn of the twenty-first century, and 45.2 points per game in the 2014 season. Scoring plays are football's most exciting moments. In 1977, there were an average of seven scoring plays each game. By 2014, the average had risen to ten. That's

---

[*] For my money, the greatest football player ever. See the note on Rice in Bonus #1.

about 30 percent more jumping out of your seat with both arms raised.

To state the defensive coordinator's perspective in haiku,[*]

> *Clipboard hurled in air:*
> *those [bleeped out] just scored again.*
> *Sideline in autumn.*

Passing records began wafting downward like dying leaves as winter approached. Eighty-seven of the top hundred NFL seasons for passing yards by a quarterback would come after the 1996 tightening of the chuck rule. Nine of the NFL's top ten passing-yards seasons followed the new rule.[†] All of the top five passing-yards seasons would come after the 2006 rules on quarterback protection. Before the 1978 rule change, NFL games were 55 percent rushing, 45 percent passing. By the 2014 season, the NFL was 59 percent passing, 41 percent rushing.[‡]

More scoring led to grumbling from the old school, but no NFL owner could fail to notice that ratings and revenue were rising. Pass-first professional football did not merely create more instances of the two-arms-raised "touchdown!" signal.

---

[*] The best-known haiku of the seventeenth-century master Basho goes like this:

On a withered branch

a crow has now alighted:

Nightfall in autumn.

[†] The increase of the regular season from fourteen to sixteen games occurred in 1978, so added contests were not the cause of these rising stats.

[‡] This is the called-passes calculation that counts pass attempts, sacks, and scrambles: situations when a passing play is what the offense intended.

Pass-first football added grace and motion to the game. Rushing the football is about strong men colliding, and a well-executed rushing play has a certain aesthetic. Passing the football is about choreography, with strength, speed and elegance combined.

Plus there's the moment when the pass is in the air and the crowd holds its collective breath. Sure, many passes clang to the ground. But when a tight spiral is soaring above a dozen athletes' heads as two sculpted men engage in a footrace to catch the ball, there's an instant of suspended time that just does not happen on a four-yard off-tackle dive.

Rule changes allowed professional football to evolve from a ground-and-pound format to an aerial circus—a "quarterback league" in the term of art that is now the consensus of scouts and touts. Nowhere was this evolution better seen than in the career of Bill Belichick, the man who personifies America's love-hate relationship with the NFL.

Belichick, whose background was coaching defense, got his big break in the NFL when he became defensive coordinator of the New York Giants in 1985. In this role, he obsessively studied defensive tactics. The defensive game plan Belichick drew up to slow the heavily favored no-huddle Buffalo Bills in the 1991 Super Bowl is now on display at Canton.

Named the New England head coach in 2000, initially Belichick attempted to build an orthodox squad—power defense, run-first offense. Concluding Belichick's second season at New England, the Patriots won the 2002 Super Bowl with what any purist would call perfect balance—an offense that rushed 50 percent of the time and passed 50 percent of the time. Belichick's traditional offense of that season took its sweet time, always huddling, staging just fifty-four snaps in the 2002 Super Bowl triumph.

Then Belichick became a convert to a core bit of sports analytics: on average, passing plays gain more yards than rushing plays. For instance, in 2014, NFL teams averaged a net of 6.4 yards per pass attempt versus 4.2 yards per rush attempt.[*] This basic ratio—passes generate about half again as much yardage as rushes—has held for many decades. In 1935, for example, the average NFL pass attempt yielded 5.2 yards, the average rush 3 yards.

The higher yield for pass attempts has long been known but tended to be dismissed by coaches, who would cite this football folk wisdom, usually attributed to Darrell Royal, the Texas Longhorns coach from 1957 to 1976: "When you throw the football three things can happen, and two of them are bad." The three things are a completion, a sack, or an interception.[†] Actually, when you run the football three things can happen as well, and two of them are bad—gain of yardage, loss of yardage or fumble. But putting the ball in the air seems intemperate while running seems cautious. For decades, many coaches felt Royal's words were all the analysis they needed.

---

[*] The passing net is yards gained on receptions minus yards lost on sacks. Yours truly has argued that interception returns should be subtracted from passing yards gained, and fumble runbacks subtracted from rushing yards gained. But the NFL doesn't keep stats this way.

[†] Actually, five things can happen—completion, incompletion, sack, interception, scramble—and three of them are bad. In the New England offense six things can happen, since occasionally Tom Brady pooch-punts from passing formation.

Pass-flavored NFL rules changes altered the Royal wisdom. In 1977, the last season before the passing-game rule changes began, 51.3 percent of NFL passing calls resulted in completions, 8.9 percent resulted in sacks and 5.7 percent resulted in interceptions. Royal's two bad things happened on 14.6 percent of passing calls. By 2014, the NFL completion percentage was 62.6 percent, the sack rate 6.3 percent and the interception share 2.5 percent. Bad things were happening only 8.8 percent of the time—while the desired result, a completion, had become more common.

Stated another way: a hundred passing calls in 1977 would yield 51 gains for the offense, 34 wasted downs (incompletions) and 15 misfortunes. By 2014, 100 passing calls yielded 63 gains for the offense, only 28 wasted downs and just 9 misfortunes. The new rules reduced the risk of airing out the ball, while increasing the reward.

What happened to rushing numbers in the same period? In 1977, the average rush gained 3.8 yards, and 2.1 percent of running-play calls resulted in fumbles. By 2014, the average rush gained 4.2 yards, with 1.3 percent of running calls leading to the runner "putting the ball on the ground." Since the rules regarding rushing have changed little, probably the mild improvement in rushing stats traces to defenders being backed off to combat the aerial tactics. Worried about the pass, contemporary NFL teams show a nickel (five defensive backs) or dime (six defensive backs) about half the time. Whenever a broad-shouldered linebacker leaves the action to be replaced by a slender defensive back, draw plays and tosses become more attractive.

While the NFL's rules were changing in many ways that favored the forward pass, something was bubbling upward from the high school level—the 7 on 7 fad. Beginning roughly around 2000, coaches in Texas, the center of prep football culture, formed 7 on 7 leagues to circumvent practice-time restrictions. The 7 on 7 version of the sport is a sophisticated form of touch football. No tackling, running plays or pass-rushing allowed: just receivers and defenders trying to stop them. The ball is snapped and the quarterback has three-Mississippi to release or officials blow the play dead and credit the defense with an incompletion. Because there are no pads and 7 on 7 can be organized without (officially, at least) the high school head coach having any involvement, practice-time limits don't apply.

Seven on seven, which has spread to many states, is a terrible development for the sociology of football, causing millions of high school boys to waste boundless hours that they might have been using to improve their GPAs or participate in extracurricular activity in order to get regular admission to college when recruiters don't come calling.

But for the tiny fraction of high school boys with NFL potential, the 7 on 7 fad has been a tremendous boon. How do you get to Carnegie Hall? Practice, practice, practice. Boys who have grown up spending their springs and summers in 7 on 7 are better at pitch-and-catch than previous generations, simply by virtue of rehearsal time. Texas-raised quarterbacks including Andy Dalton of Cincinnati, Nick Foles of St. Louis, Robert Griffin III of Washington, Andrew Luck of Indianapolis and Ryan Tannehill of Miami, members of the inaugural 7-on-7 generation, quickly became NFL starters in no small part because as youngsters they threw thousands more passes than young quarterbacks of prior generations.

Rolling together rules changes and the increasing emphasis on the pass at the prep and college levels produces the remarkable stat that the NFL's 2014 average completion percentage was 62.6 percent. That 62.6 percentage—the average completion percentage, including crummy quarterbacks on cover-your-eyes awful teams—was higher than the career completion numbers posted by modern-era Hall of Fame quarterbacks Troy Aikman, Terry Bradshaw, Len Dawson, John Elway, Dan Fouts, Bob Griese, Sonny Jurgensen, Jim Kelly, Dan Marino, Warren Moon, Joe Namath, Bart Starr, Roger Staubach and Fran Tarkenton. The 2014 completion average was higher than the career percentage for Brett Favre, who might possibly make the Hall of Fame. Several NFL quarterbacks who in 2014 were benched, including Brian Hoyer and Josh McCown, had a higher completion percentage than Hall of Famer Johnny Unitas. In 2014, there were seventeen NFL quarterbacks, including St. Louis emergency substitute Austin Davis, with a better completion percentage than Hall of Famer Joe Montana, winner of four Super Bowls. Davis was a walk-on in college—no recruiting offers—then undrafted by the NFL. He'd been waived by two NFL teams when the Rams turned to him because of injuries to their starter and his understudy. A who-dat dragged in off the street proceeded to post a better completion percentage than Joe Montana.[*] That is recent NFL rule changes in a nutshell.

---

[*] In the 1980s, Montana ran the 49ers' West Coast Offense, a strategy built on high percentage short passes. What was high percentage a generation ago would, by today's rules, be average.

Belichick realized a web of changes—rules that encourage passing plays, young players who'd spent huge amounts of time in youth practicing passing—constituted an argument to "hurl that spheroid down the field," as Tom Lehrer would say.[*] Around the same time, college football was swept by the quick-snap craze. That meant new players arriving for Patriots' tryouts already were versed in the quirks of the quick-snap. So Belichick changed the Patriots' offense from traditional to hurry-up pass-wacky.

By the 2007 season, when New England reached the Super Bowl at 18-0, the Patriots had what was then the NFL's highest-scoring offense ever—and were throwing almost twice as often as they ran. By the 2013 season, when New England set an all-time record for total first downs, the Patriots were staging an unprecedented average of 71 snaps per contest.[†] Belichick had adopted college-perfected uptempo tricks such as having the receiver who catches the pass run the ball over to an official, so the ready-to-play signal can be given more quickly. A fast, no-huddle pace meant more snaps; high-percentage passing meant more first downs; more first downs led

---

[*] The best football fight songs are Lehrer's Fight Fiercely Harvard, written in 1945, and Al Yankovic's Sports Song, from 2013. Both can be listened to on YouTube. Lehrer sample lyric: "How we will celebrate our victory/We shall invite the whole team up for tea!" Most Yankovic ditties are lampoons of well-known pop hits. Sports Song is original, and he performs it backed by a full marching band. Sample lyric: "What's the use of even going through the motions/when you know that you're gonna lose anyhow/so why don't you save us all some time and give up now."

[†] Many college programs have an even higher average: the Oregon Ducks averaged 82 snaps in 2014, for instance. NCAA clock-operator standards are written to maximize the number of plays per game.

to more touchdowns. And the object of the game is, after all, to score the most points.

There are vogues in sports just as in fashion and music, and the NFL's pass-pass-pass vogue may have peaked in 2012, when the Giants won the Super Bowl despite finishing last in rushing. Two seasons later, the Broncos, behind Peyton Manning, became the all-time highest scoring team, and set the record for most total touchdowns, employing an offense that passed 60 percent of the time—then were decisively defeated in the Super Bowl by the Seattle Seahawks, who used a conventional grind-it-out running offense. In that Super Bowl-winning season, the Seahawks ran more often than they threw. This indicated a pendulum beginning to swing back.

Even if the next fad is for balanced offense, higher-scoring football seems here to stay. High-scoring games are a lot more fun for the national television audience. Increased passing proficiency and higher ratings amplify each other.

The NFL evolution that began in the late 1970s had other components that improved quality of play. Orthopedic medicine made rapid strides. Knee injuries that once would have ended an athletic career, or resulted in surgery that ruined a player's speed, gave way to minimally invasive arthroscopic procedures with good results. The two torn knee ligaments that Adrian Peterson suffered the day after Christmas 2011 would have been lights-out for a football star of a generation ago. Nine months later Peterson was back on the field at full strength; he had a magnificent 2012 season and won the NFL MVP award. Spectators want to see the best players. Increasingly, orthopedic advances keep that possible.

Developments in sports medicine and exercise science boosted NFL quality. Nautilus-style exercise equipment, which hit the market in the 1970s, allows athletes to build muscle mass without the old problem of loss of flexibility. Lifting free weights changed from old-fashioned grunt-and-strain to controlled routines aimed at muscle exhaustion in a planned sequence. Gatorade improved hydration, which is deceptively important both for athletic performance and for safety. The 2001 training-camp death from heat stroke of Minnesota Vikings tackle Korey Stringer woke up coaches at all levels to the need for plenty of fluids, and plenty of shade breaks, during August heat.*

Around the same time, fitness specialists became more aware of the role of aerobic conditioning. Football players had always done calisthenics: now they began jogging, taking Denise-Austin-style aerobics classes, seeking an edge through yoga or ballet instruction. Games of the 1950s were slugfests, victory going to whichever team still could stand up in the fourth quarter. Once football players were both strong and aerobically fit, quality of play improved.

Beyond new rules and improved health care, the economic structure of the NFL was changing in a way that favored better games. Back in the day, playing professional football was an

---

* Heat stroke death is 100 percent preventable in any controlled setting, including football two-a-days. High school coaches and state athletic associations were too slow to recognize this. It took twelve years, from the 2001 warning bell sounded by Stringer's death, till 2013, for all states to mandate summer heat-management standards for football practice. Thirty-four high school football players died of heat stroke during this period when states were dragging their feet on imposing August restrictions.

avocation—even stars had off-season jobs. Adjusting to current dollars, the average NFL salary of the 1950s was about $40,000, below today's median household income. Then, players could not afford to spend the off-season lifting, doing drills and honing their football skills. When Lou Groza was a nine-time Pro Bowl performer for the Cleveland Browns of the 1950s through the 1960s, he sold life insurance during the off-season. Teammate Chuck Noll, later to coach the Pittsburgh Steelers to four Super Bowl trophies, worked as an account rep for a trucking company. Noll and Groza were stars: the lesser-known took construction jobs or labored in warehouses. To this day the ten-man NFL junior varsity unit—reserves who provide the regulars with someone to practice against, who don't dress on Sunday and who dream of promotion to the gameday roster—is known as the taxi squad. The name harks back to when NFL players worked as cabbies to make ends meet.

By the time of the 1978 Super Bowl, the NFL average salary had risen to $360,000. Now a job in the NFL allowed players to condition and watch film year-round. By 1993, the year the NFL union won free agency for members and also switched to cooperative bargaining, the average NFL player made $1.3 million. For 2015, the average is about $2.4 million.* Too many NFL players live large and end up declaring bankruptcy, care-

---

* The first NFL salary cap, in 1994, was $56 million. In 2015, the cap was $143 million. That's a 155 percent increase in money to players, versus a 152 percent increase in money to NBA players in the same period and an 89 percent MLB increase. About 90 percent of the NFL salary cap goes to active players, the balance to pensions and health care for former players.

lessness with money being a special hazard in a profession where the average "career" is around four years.* But for the last quarter-century, professional football has paid enough that its players can be full-time professionals. This has been another boon to gameday quality.

By the twenty-first century, many factors—rule changes, rising player income, improved sports medicine—conjoined to cause NFL games to become steadily better. Technology put the more exciting contest everywhere—on high-definition flat screens in dens, taverns and restaurants; on laptops and tablets; on smartphones.

Video games, first stand-alone, then linked via broadband, drew into football's artificial universe large numbers who'd never held a pigskin themselves, nor rooted for a hometown favorite. John Madden is in the Hall of Fame not so much for his coaching achievements, since thirty-five men have more career victories,† but for his role in EA's video game franchise. The first Madden NFL video game, released in 1988 for use on

---

* In most NFL contracts, little future money is guaranteed. If a player's performance declines owing to injury, or simply to the cumulative effect of years of being pounded by muscular, ill-tempered opponents, the team can cancel the remainder of the deal. Little more than a token severance and cab fare to the airport is owed. NFL players rightly complain that if they have a bad year or sustain a bad injury, their deals are ripped up and essentially they are fired: while if they "outperform their contract" by playing better than expected, owners lecture them about the sanctity of honoring the rest of the agreement.

† Buddy Parker, of whom most football zealots have never heard, coached more NFL wins than Madden. Ahead of Madden on the career-victories metric are Dennis Green and Norv Turner, both widely viewed as dismal head coaches.

a Commodore 64,[*] spawned an annual iteration of increasing depth and fidelity, including the voices of network announcers and avatars based on "performance capture" digitization of the actual players.

The advent and popularity of fantasy football was the cherry on the sundae: to fantasy league members, even an otherwise lackluster pairing of two losing teams can have significance.

A sign of the times was that the old pattern of disappointing Super Bowls gave way to the Super Bowl being terrific. At this writing, six of the last eight Super Bowls have been the best game of the season. Three of the last four Super Bowls came down to the trailing team reaching goal-to-go with seconds remaining.

What's the best part of a fireworks display? The finale, of course.

"Save the best for last" is a long-standing formula for entertainment-industry success. The NFL might generate controversy, even waves of negativity. But terrific games leading up to a terrific Super Bowl leave a sweet aftertaste, with the audience longing for more.

---

[*] The latest smartphones have fifteen hundred times the processing power and two million times the memory of a Commodore.

# You Ain't Seen Nothin' Yet

The NFL has expanded from twenty-six teams playing 189 games in 1970 to thirty-two teams playing 267 games in 2015. That's 41 percent more action—Major League Baseball has seen a 26 percent games-played increase in the same period. Attendance at NFL contests has grown from 9.9 million in 1970 to 17.3 million in 2014. Broadcasting has expanded from one game per week to five to seven per week depending on the time of year. The small minority of Americans whose dwellings receive NFL Sunday Ticket may skim around to as many as sixteen games weekly.* The larger group with access to NFL Network's Red Zone Channel sees live-action highlights from every contest. NFL ratings have grown from decent to 800-pound-gorilla class, with the most-watched TV events in the United States all being Super Bowls.† Some seventy-six million people watched the *Seinfeld*

---

* See Chapter eight for details on how NFL Sunday Ticket was designed to screw the typical fan.

† If it's any consolation, in Denmark the annual men's handball championship draws about the same share of TV viewers as the Super Bowl draws in the United States.

finale; 168 million watched the 2015 Super Bowl. NBC's *Sunday Night Football* has for several years been entrenched as the top-rated show on television.[*] The typical NFL game in 2014 drew seventeen million viewers, better than the viewership of *Game of Thrones* and way better than the one million who tuned in to the typical NBA showdown.

As for money—the government of Greece can only dream of the NFL's command of money. Thirty years ago, the NFL's three broadcast partners paid the league about $900 million per year in rights fees to air games. In 2015, the NFL's broadcast partners—AT&T/DirecTV, CBS, ESPN, Fox, NBC, NFL Network, Verizon and Yahoo— paid $7.8 billion in rights fees to air games.[†] That's nearly nine times as much as three decades ago. Broadcast-rights deals begin to expire in 2021. A bidding war is expected then, if not sooner.

Sponsorship agreements up the totals. Current sponsors including Anheuser Busch, Hyundai, Papa John's, Pepsi and Visa pay the league about $1.2 billion annually to use the NFL logo.[‡] Future historians may scratch their heads about why CoverGirl sponsors this most masculine of sports: nevertheless, CoverGirl does, paying the NFL for the right to run advertisements of fashion models in football helmets wearing elaborate eye

---

[*] In 2014-2015 ratings, *Sunday Night Football* bested the surprise hit *Empire* by a small margin while clobbering *The Voice, American Idol, Grey's Anatomy,* the countless *NCIS* variants, and other ratings stalwarts.

[†] Though NFL Network is league-owned, it bids for the Thursday night games against other carriers.

[‡] The NFL also takes a fee from the USAA insurance company to allow USAA to call itself the "Official Military Appreciation Sponsor of the NFL," a phrase that sounds impressive but is nearly meaningless.

makeup in jersey colors of the Broncos, Dolphins, Seahawks and other teams. Business professors may wonder if it can really be worth $23 million a year to Gatorade to have bottles of Citrus Cooler Extremo on pro football sidelines; Gatorade thinks so. Corporate America appears to have nearly unlimited enthusiasm for the NFL.

Add in local sponsorships, stadium naming rights, apparel sales and other marketing and the NFL garners about $12 billion per year,[*] near to the GDP of Iceland. Did we forget ticket sales? Until a generation ago, pro football was dependent for revenue on placing rear ends into seats. This was the reason owners insisted that games with unsold tickets be blacked out on local television. Today, the NFL revenue base is national television and, increasingly, the Internet, boosted by national marketing. Spinning the turnstiles at stadium gates is nice but not essential, which explains why the NFL is content with franchises in Green Bay and Jacksonville, while much larger cities go untapped.

The ratings and money, joined to pro football's outsized role in American culture and politics, would seem to make it impossible for the NFL to get any bigger. But at each previous stage it seemed the NFL could not get any bigger, and it did. The same may happen again.

---

[*] The exact figure is not known because with the exception of the Green Bay Packers, NFL clubs are closely-held family firms, not required to disclose financial data. The publicly owned Packers' report of $376 million in 2014 revenue puts the league-wide total at about $12 billion, with a greater sum expected for 2015. A number of NFL owners are known to want the Packers converted into a closely-held private firm so they would not announce numbers: then nothing at all about NFL finances would be disclosed.

Further growth may come through the simple expedient of more kickoffs. Currently, the NFL stages 256 regular season games followed by eleven postseason contests. That's a steep increase compared to 1970, when 182 regular season dates were followed by seven postseason confrontations. But why stop at the current total?

The paucity of NFL playoff games has long troubled the networks, if not purists. All the NFL hoopla builds to a mere eleven postseason events, none during Monday through Thursday prime time, peak period for viewership. In 2015, the NBA staged 63 playoff contests, most during weeknight prime time. There's a lot of airtime crying out to be filled by NFL playoffs.

That NFL postseason contests are few is part of what makes each game exciting and memorable. Tampering with that might dilute the NFL's remarkable product quality. But more playoff games also would mean more money: When the very rich are given a choice between quality and cash, what do you suppose is likely? If additional playoff games were slated, that would represent extra dessert following the NFL main course. Schedules might be jiggered to place playoff contests into weeknight prime time.

Most NFL owners back expansion to an eighteen-game regular season, either by eliminating two of the four current preseason contests or by keeping all four and adding two real games. Players and coaches uniformly dislike the four meaningless preseason games; television audiences are indifferent; and season-ticket holders abhor them, as teams require season-ticket buyers to purchase the two irrelevant August home games in order to attend the eight real games.

The Santa Fe Opera doesn't invite men in tuxedos and women in evening gowns to preseason oeuvres with backup divas, and the American Ballet Theater doesn't stage preseason choreography performed by dancers who will be put on waivers the following day. Broadway shows offer preview performances, with tickets either discounted or distributed free ("papering the house"), allowing performers to become accustomed to audience reactions. If Broadway previews were priced like NFL preseason games, audiences at the preview would be hit up for full price for their seat and also be required to purchase a full-season subscription.

To phrase the NFL situation in haiku,

> *Fumbles, dropped passes:*
> *teams should pay crowds to attend*
> *the preseason games.*

If two preseason games are deleted and replaced by two regular season contests, injuries are likely to increase. Preseason games are played at half-speed, with starters leaving by intermission. Should two preseason contests become games that count in the standings, starters will be on the field going all-out. More wear-and-tear on players' bodies will be inevitable.

The league's leadership thinks America is eager for a longer NFL season. Roger Goodell, a proponent of the eighteen-game format, said in 2009, "We have not found a saturation point for pro football." That may be so—but wouldn't it be preferable never to discover the saturation point?

More regular season games would spawn more advertising minutes to sell plus more who-cares contests. As is, by Thanksgiving, the meetings between eliminated teams can get tedious: the 2014 season December pairing of Tennessee and Jacksonville, with a combined record of 4-24 at kickoff, was not for the faint of heart. Imagine if Thanksgiving arrived, many NFL teams were already eliminated, and the regular season still had two months remaining.

Should the NFL expand to eighteen regular season dates plus fourteen postseason invitation cards, that adds up to 60 percent more contests than in 1970. The Nonstop Football League would be distressingly near. Those who don't care for football may find the following statistic hard to believe, but there are thirty-one weeks of the year without NFL games that count in the standings, twenty-one with. Two more regular-season weeks would shift the ratio to 29-23. If preseason, the draft and the hype period of training camp weeks are included, we'd reach the situation of more weeks with the NFL than without. Even red-blooded Americans might say, *Enough already!*

The Nonstop Football League will come closer to being realized should the NFL expand again. There is no shortage of talented, ripped, eager young men. Each spring about three thousand players depart from the major-college football programs—only about half of them graduating, but that's another issue. About five hundred of the former collegians have some reasonable shot at joining the NFL, and about one hundred fifty each year succeed. That leaves plenty of able bodies to stock more NFL teams.

The Rule of 90/90 controls NFL rosters—90 percent of the fans have no idea who 90 percent of the players are. The New England Patriots just won the Super Bowl: Which of their offensive linemen can you name without peeking at the Internet? Which of their linebackers? If NFL expansion to thirty-six teams means unknowns suiting up for the Las Vegas Blackjacks or the Portland Bongs, so long as each team signs a couple of aging stars, it won't matter that the remainder of the roster is who-dat.

The NFL stages annual contests in England—one club home team of record though performing thousands of miles from home—and has attempted to win a beachhead in the continental sector of the European Union. Expansion of the NFL beyond North America seems unlikely, though many appealing franchise names would be left on the table. The London Blitz. The Frankfurt Bankers. The Edinburgh Fringe. The Brussels Sprouts. The Tel Aviv Reubens. The Warsaw Buzz Saw.* The Istanbul Intrigue. The Kiev Chickens.

Expansion cities in North America are another matter— easily imagined, regardless of what may happen with the NFL in Los Angeles. Portland and San Antonio are boomtowns. Toronto is the fourth-largest city in North America, Montreal the ninth-largest. (Canadians love the CFL but would be over the moon to have NFL franchises.) Mexico City is the continent's

---

\* My all-time favorite football team name was that of the 1928 NFL champion, the Providence Steam Roller. The name was singular, like today's Stanford Cardinal, and inexplicably, the Steam Roller logo was a dog.

largest metropolis. The NFL is a lot more popular in Mexico than in the United Kingdom. An NFL franchise called, say, the Mexico City Aztecs would nudge millions of Latino-Americans from soccer toward football as their favorite sport.

Pro football has mixed feelings about Las Vegas. It was half a century ago that NFL stars Alex Karras and Paul Hornung were caught betting on games and hanging out with mobsters. The NFL's institutional memory still considers this a traumatic moment, and shies from Vegas as a result.

There is a principled argument against gambling, which is that games of chance prey upon those with money problems. The tiny number who win big prizes creates an illusion that gambling is a path to wealth. For most, even when an element of skill is involved, gambling is a path to a repossessed house. Americans lost $119 billion gambling in 2013, twice as much as California spent on Medicaid that year. The largest chunk of losses were from state-run lotteries, which are marketed mainly in low-income zip codes. Two-thirds of state lotto wagering is by persons in the bottom quintile for income: the Powerball machine is in the liquor store, not the Whole Foods. It is deeply misanthropic for state governments to use lottos to lure the poor and working poor into handing over what cash they possess, in return for a few minutes of dreaming that their money problems are about to end.*

But principled arguments may be cast aside when money is

---

* "Funding education" is a cynical cover story for state lottos. For example, the Maryland state lotto in FY2015 directed just 28 percent of revenue to education. The median low-income player lost $425 that fiscal year. Local media organizations look the other way because state lottos are major advertisers.

waved, and considerable money is being waved in sports gambling. At least $100 million was wagered in Vegas on the Patriots-Seahawks Super Bowl. Those bets required physically being in the city—imagine how the action would grow if anyone could bet legally on the Super Bowl from a smartphone. Jason Logan, of the gambling Web site Covers, wrote in February 2015, "If you ask Nevada sportsbooks which is the most popular sport to bet, they'll tell you the NFL. If you ask them what the fastest growing sport is to bet, you'll get the same answer."

In 2014, the NBA endorsed national legalization of sports wagering. So many NBA teams make halfhearted efforts, or even deliberately lose—at this point the NBA could have an Eastern Conference, a Western Conference and a Tanking Conference—that it would be hard to tell if NBA games were being thrown. By endorsing legal sports wagering, NBA commissioner Adam Silver essentially said that sustaining the integrity of competition in basketball was less important than getting a cut of gambling proceeds.

Nevada already draws significant tax revenue from the legal sports wagering within its borders, with a total of about $4 billion bet on NFL and NBA contests in 2014. New Jersey wants to legalize sports gambling, in order to tax it: many states, and the federal government, may soon seek taxes on sports action. Big corporate entities that traditionally look askance at gambling may change their minds as government and the NBA legitimize this means of picking people's pockets.

As for the NFL, remembering Karras and Hornung, the league would punish any players or coaches betting on pro football. But the NFL does not hesitate to lease team logos and trademarks to numerous state lotteries, in return for a taste of the money pilfered from the poor. If there were a way for the NFL to receive a cut of football gambling without its players and coaches being compromised, the league might jump.

Pro football expansion into Las Vegas could be one means to combine the NFL with bookmaking. Vegas offers an intersection of Hollywood and music industry celebrities with glamour, glitz and an anything-can-be-arranged-for-a-price mindset. If showgirls staffed the cheerleader squad of the NFL's expansion Las Vegas Sinners, that's another draw.

More appealing to the NFL than Las Vegas expansion may be the action on the Web. Fantasy football, since the proliferation of broadband a big factor in rising attention paid to the NFL, has begun merging with gambling. Web sites such as Fan Duel are, on paper, fantasy leagues, but in effect are roulette wheels—"over $10 million in cash prizes paid out each week," Fan Duel promises. The venture-investing arms of Comcast and Time Warner put $275 million into Fan Duel in 2015, while the venture arm of Fox Sports led a $300 million underwriting round for Draft Kings, the other leading fantasy-qua-gambling Web site. About the same time, ESPN signed an exclusive advertising deal with Draft Kings, meaning Fox and ESPN both now share a financial stake in encouraging gambling on the NFL.*

In summer 2015, Yahoo became the latest big corporation to partner with the NFL, winning a contract to live-stream the

---

* Fan Duel, Draft Kings and imitator sites offer gambling on many sports, but pro football is the most popular. Betting surges when the NFL season kicks off.

league's London contests. Almost immediately after inking this agreement, Yahoo announced a football "fantasy" division that is all but officially a sports book.

That Yahoo, the NFL's newest corporate partner, supports gambling on the NFL may be a harbinger. NFL clubs could have both a will-call window for tickets and a betting window for laying wagers. The NFL could post its own point spreads and charge a membership fee for using the Official Bookie of the NFL. Season-ticket holders could receive an automatic 0.5 points added to their bets for or against the spread. High rollers could pay to receive insider info from coaches. Not just point-spread bets but over/under and proposition wagers could be administered by the NFL directly. Punters could place wagers on punters!

Regardless of what may happen with sports wagering—I'm offering two-to-one odds that the above paragraph someday will not sound like satire—pro football is likely to continue to become bigger both sociologically and economically. One scenario is NFL expansion to thirty-six teams playing eighteen regular season contests followed by a sixteen-team postseason bracket. That would add up to 340 consequential NFL games—80 percent more than in 1970.

The public may or may not be demanding more NFL contests—but television executives are, and this could be the determining aspect.

With the television world atomized by DVRs and online viewing, there's steadily less incentive to make popcorn, sit on the couch and follow along live. Increasingly, the content that cable carriers push into the family television may be watched for less, or for no charge, on the broadband and wi-fi systems that millennials pay for in any case. Why use the cable carriers as middlemen for the monthly payment they pass along to the big-four networks, when those networks air their content free on phones and laptops? Maybe you stick with cable to stay in touch with the news. But do you really need to send Comcast $75 a month to beam CNN into your TV, when you could wait a few minutes and get the story—plus video—on the *New York Times* Web site?

That leaves sports. In the cord-cutting era, the strongest argument for a cable bill is live sports. In turn, pro football is the most popular sport. That leaves the NFL as the salvation not just for the cable industry, but for the networks whose business model relies on the pass-along of monthly fees collected by cable carriers. Big as the NFL has been on television in the last generation, it's likely to get bigger in the next. CBS, Fox and NBC—and ABC indirectly via its sister channel, ESPN—may cling to the NFL for survival.

While the marketing of cable now favors live sports over other visual content, the economics of television favor sports over sitcoms and dramas, too. Advertising rates for NFL games are almost always higher than for scripted or reality programming. *Monday Night Football* sells advertising time for an average of about $400,000 per 30 seconds—about double the rate of anything else on TV on Monday evenings. Routine Sunday afternoon contests sell advertising at up to $250,000 per 30 seconds—versus the final season of *Breaking Bad*, a hullabalooed TV event, selling ads for around $175,000 per 30 seconds. The 2015 Super Bowl brought NBC about $4.2 million per 30 seconds. CBS hopes Super Bowl 50 will break the $5 million barrier.*

Television economics favor football over shows in other ways. One is production price per hour. Typically, an hour of a scripted prime-time television show costs around $2 million to produce; the flashy final season of *Breaking Bad* cost about $3.5 million per episode. That's versus about $1 million to produce a Sunday afternoon NFL game and about $2 million to produce a night game. (*Sunday Night Football* and *Monday Night Football* offer more camera angles and game-specific material than daylight contests.) Rights fees that are folded into the production cost of scripted shows must be added to sports programming. But if scripted-show production costs $2 million for one hour while NFL game production is $1 million for three hours, and the NFL advertising rates are higher, which will a network prefer?

Beneath the surface are the venture-capital aspects of television. Pilots for half-hour sitcoms cost about $2 million to make; pilots for hour-long drama shows, even yet another formulaic police procedural, may cost $5 million. But the majority of pilots never become a series. So for each debut prime-time show in a network's annual upfronts—say, a spinoff called *NCIS: Spinoff* or a reality show in which contestants are trapped on the sound stage of a reality show—there may be $50 million to $100 million of failed pilots. That's a hidden sunk cost for the series that actually air.

Sports, by contrast, do not have any pilot-episode expense.

---

* In Super Bowl terms that would be $V million per XXX seconds.

There's no need to invent an NFL premise every year, develop it in scriptwriters' meetings, screen-test actors, build sets, go on location shoots, tediously negotiate a dozen "produced by" credits for Hollywood grandees who will never actually glance at the script. On the day the NFL season kicks off, the sunk cost to reach that juncture is zero.

In turn, the NFL will never be cancelled. Many prime-time series don't make the end of the first season: a three-season run is a success. The CBS drama *Madam Secretary*, which debuted in fall 2014, is an expensive show with a big cast, complex sets and a combination of actual location shooting and faux location shoots. (That scene may have looked like it happened in Iran....) The series opened with fifteen million viewers, a strong number, tailing off to ten million by what was supposed to be the shocking cliffhanger season finale. If *Madam Secretary* runs seven seasons, as *The West Wing* did, CBS will be very happy. If the show is cancelled during or following its second year, a large amount of pilot and production money will swirl down the drain.

This doesn't happen with NFL games. There will always be a next season.

That the NFL grows steadily more important to the survival of major TV networks, and of cable carriers, explains the stratospheric rise of the NFL's television rights fees. Such payments have grown from $900 million per year three decades ago, to $1.7 billion per year two decades ago, to $4 billion per year one decade ago, to $7.8 billion per year today. The progression is nearly arithmetic, suggesting the fees will double again, to $15 billion a year, within a decade.

Today, ESPN pays $1.9 billion annually to the NFL to broadcast a mere eighteen games, seventeen on Mondays plus a postseason date—a stunning $106 million per contest.* (Fox pays MLB about $5 million for each of the roughly hundred games it airs.) That huge ESPN NFL fee works out to about $330,000 annually from ESPN to each athlete on an NFL roster. The next time a pro football player such as Marshawn Lynch throws a hissy fit about having to answer some mind-numbing question from an ESPN microphone-holder, he should bear in mind how much the Bristol-based company places directly into his pocket.

The $1.9 billion check Bristol mails to NFL headquarters each season is somewhat deceptive in that it includes rights fees for 365/24/7 airing of NFL highlights on the many talk shows that ESPN uses to fill airtime. Pro football highlights make the shows more appealing.† Sportsyak is to ESPN what jumbo sodas are to convenience stores: a big container of cheap ingredients, mostly fizz and sweetener, that's all markup.

In return for the $1.9 billion, the NFL thanks ESPN by, year after year, awarding the company a slate of substandard games.

---

* ESPN pays about $90 million per game for the seven top college football bowl contests. The inaugural year of the big college football playoff bracket had fabulous viewership, suggesting ESPN locked in a good price. Big-college football ratings and viewer numbers are so strong that NFL-sized rights fees may be coming down the road.

† Whether the NFL ought to be able to charge for highlights—that is, whether pro sports leagues should be able to copyright images created in publicly funded stadia—is addressed in detail in my 2013 book *The King of Sports*.

NBC, network of *Sunday Night Football*, pays the NFL about $950 million annually, about half what is paid by the network of *Monday Night Football*. Suppose we compared the 2015 slates the league drew up for NBC and ESPN. Every season, some team expected to be good does a nosedive, and every season, an underdog emerges. So there's always a game that seems important before the season starts and turns out not to be, always a game expected to be a dog that turns out to be a jewel. To adjust for such unknowns, we'll compare the 2015 *Sunday Night Football* and *Monday Night Football* slates using only the information available to the NFL at the time the schedules were drawn up in winter 2015: namely, who made the playoffs after the 2014 season, and which franchises have in recent years been the subject of strong ratings or fan interest.

For eighteen *Sunday Night Football* contests entailing thirty-six total NFL representatives, NBC received twenty-six appearances by playoff teams from the previous season, or 72 percent high-quality teams. The majority of NBC's games—ten of eighteen—paired two playoff teams from the previous season.[*] NBC got rematches of both conference title games from the previous season; twelve total appearances by the league's glamour clubs (Denver, Green Bay, New England and Seattle); and three appearances by the Dallas Cowboys, the NFL's most reliable ratings draw. Just two games on the NBC slate paired weak teams from the previous season. Not to worry: NBC's contract

---

[*] By the time you read this, one of those pairings may have turned from monster into laffer. Bear in mind, this section is based on what was known when the schedule was composed.

allows it to "flex" twice a season, dropping a pairing that turns out to be uninteresting in favor of a strong matchup originally scheduled as a daylight contest.

Now let's look at the *Monday Night Football* 2015 slate of seventeen games, or thirty-four total NFL representatives. Only sixteen appearances, 47 percent, are by playoff teams from the previous season. A small minority—four of the seventeen contests—pairs two playoff teams from the previous season. There's no rematch of a postseason contest from the prior season. ESPN gets only four total appearances by the league's Glam Four and only one Cowboys date. *Monday Night Football*, in 2015, offers woofers as far as the eye can see, including five games pairing teams that both failed to reach the postseason the prior year. To top things off, ESPN does not get to "flex" bad games into good ones, as NBC can.

Bottom line: ESPN pays the NFL twice as much as NBC pays and is rewarded with a second-rate schedule. The company that calls itself the Worldwide Leader in Sports—is it daft?

Probably, but not for this reason. ESPN would like a stronger slate of games, but what matters to the company is making money, and the NFL arrangement is very effective in that regard. ESPN attains use of NFL highlights year-round, which has more value to a sports-channel empire than to NBC. Moreover, the NFL is ESPN's anchor for cable fees that are tops in the industry.

Cable carriers pay ESPN about $6 per month per household, an order of magnitude higher than the roughly $1.50 per month cable carriers pay for TNT, the second-most expensive cable offering. Six dollars per month multiplied by ninety-three million households adds up to nearly $7 billion in annual revenue for ESPN.* This sum is by far the shiniest treasure chest in cable's pirate ship: CNN gets 62 cents per subscriber per month, about a tenth of what ESPN receives.

Consumer advocates protest that basic cable, the most common cable package, is structured so as to compel consumers to buy ESPN—paying more for sports than they pay for news. (CNN, Fox News and MSNBC combined cost the typical cable customer about a dollar a month.) The roughly $7 billion ESPN collects annually from cable fees imposed on consumers whether they like sports or not is a huge hidden subsidy from average people to the billionaires who own professional franchises and the millionaires who play for them. If the basic-cable concept—a prepackaged set of channels—were replaced with a la carte ordering, enabling customers to decide for themselves whether they wanted to pay $72 a year for ESPN, many would say yes: I certainly would. But many would not. ESPN would become less of a money machine, billionaires would accumulate less, spectacular sports salaries would edge downward, and bidding wars for sports programming rights would cool.

Potential loss of subscriber-fee revenue from basic cable is ESPN's biggest corporate worry. The moat around ESPN's cable-fees arrangement is the NFL. As is, cable carriers try only to bargain ESPN's fee downward: no cable carrier wants to drop ESPN and tell customers, "Sorry, we don't offer *Monday*

---

* ESPN realizes about $3 billion per annum on TV advertising and about $1 billion annually from Web site ads, meaning that while most networks gain most revenue from advertising, ESPN gains about twice as much from cable subscriber fees as from ads.

*Night Football.*" This is why ESPN does not complain about being handed a slate of woofer games while NBC pays half as much for better pairings. ESPN's priority is maintaining the cable-package status quo, and the NFL is essential for that.

Beyond the difference between cable and over-the-air TV economics is a larger tension: the National Football League loathes Entertainment and Sports Programming Network.

The reasons are many, one simply money. When the league started NFL Network a little more than a decade ago, the plan was to attack ESPN head-to-head and haul in some of the cable subscriber fee treasure chest. When that didn't work, the NFL engaged in discussions about buying ESPN or joint-venturing with Bristol. That didn't work either. Today, the NFL stares at the $7 billion in cable subscriber fees ESPN enjoys, stares at ESPN's very successful Web presence (world's #29 site compared to NFL.com at #421 globally) and feels covetous. It's not the kind of feeling that promotes harmony.

A dalliance in the NFL-ESPN relationship was the 2003 TV series *Playmakers*, ESPN's attempt at scripted television. *Playmakers* depicted a thinly disguised NFL in which drugs are ubiquitous, athletes mistreat women, owners are children throwing tantrums and football stars are viewed by team management as glorified oxen. That is to say, *Playmakers* sugarcoated the actual situation. NFL owners went into a nuclear meltdown at the realization that the country's leading sports network was running a show making the country's leading sport look bad. The NFL pressured ESPN to cancel the series after its initial season.

Early in ESPN's existence, the NFL was grateful for the

THE GAME'S NOT OVER

innovations created by the network. Airing the NFL draft was ESPN's idea: this 1980 decision, then viewed as ludicrous, led to what is now a significant source of promotion for the league. Not only did ESPN put the announcement of unknown names on the air—"with the 138th choice of the 1980 NFL draft, the Pittsburgh Steelers take guard Craig Wolfley, Syracuse"—but ESPN handed a commentator's chair to Mel Kiper, Jr. Kiper was unlike anything sports television previously had seen: manic, obsessive-compulsive and willing to mock NFL scouts and general managers. His presence legitimized what had till then been an underground of draftniks: this was good for the NFL and also helped set the stage for the fantasy sports explosion.

During its initial years, ESPN offered two important football coverage innovations, *Primetime* and *SportsCenter*. *Primetime* was a full hour packed with rapid-fire NFL highlights—not just touchdowns but sacks, draw plays, tosses, incomplete passes. Obsolete today owing to highlights in real-time, *Primetime* educated viewers, was entertaining, and established the idea—then strange, now customary—that just because the day's contests had concluded didn't mean fans should stop watching.

*SportsCenter* brought a city desk mentality, creating a new concept of what to watch before bed: you didn't tune in to the local newscast to hear about fires, crimes and weather; you watched *SportsCenter* present athletics as news. Like *Primetime*, *SportsCenter* had a sense of humor: till these two shows, coverage of football was deathly serious. *Primetime* and *SportsCenter* treated football as a source of amusement. This outlook caught on, to the NFL's benefit.

But much as the NFL's expansion in ratings and money was aided by ESPN, hard feelings developed. Many NFL owners are spoiled and egotistical: they believe themselves the last of the Habsburgs, and expect to be treated as royalty.* News coverage on *SportsCenter* and on ESPN's high-quality, if low-profile, public-affairs show *Outside the Lines* caused owners to pull out what hair they had. The NFL's other broadcast partners—CBS, Fox and NBC—ritually kiss the ring of the league. When NFL owners watched hard-hitting sports coverage on ESPN while the NFL on CBS, Fox, and NBC was cotton candy; when the owners encountered detailed, sophisticated and original criticism of the NFL on ESPN.com: owners wondered, whose side are they on anyway?

There is nothing the NFL can do about reproach from organizations with which it does not partner—the league can't touch the *Washington Post, The Atlantic* or independent Web sites. But the league can pressure any partners to produce only happy talk. As the money rises, pressure from the NFL ratchets up. Merely during the decade when I penned Tuesday Morning Quarterback for ESPN, Bristol's financial commitment to the NFL doubled while pro football became a significant profit center for Disney and Hearst, ESPN's owners.† Each time the

---

\* The NFL owners' view of themselves as majestic titans astride the landscape—rather than as people who got lucky by investing in a nice sport—is another way in which pro football holds a mirror to American society. Luck is a huge factor in life. But the rich want to believe they are rich, and others poor, because they have superhuman merit and others do not.

† Because the movie business scatters money to the four winds while ESPN runs a tight ship, ESPN provides Disney with about 15 percent of its revenue but about 25 percent of its profit.

money at stake increases, so too does the temptation to cave. ESPN was the last holdout of independent thinking among NFL broadcast partners, and, by 2015, seemed to be running up the white flag, in a short span offloading Bill Simmons, Keith Olbermann and TMQ, its three strongest voices questioning NFL priorities.* Coincidence? Maybe.

In 2015, a senior executive of an NFL network partner other than ESPN told me, "We can't allow our writers or broadcasters free reign regarding the NFL anymore, and we are not proud of this. So much money has started flowing through the NFL, while pro football has become so crucial because ratings for everything except the NFL are down, that we are now completely terrified of upsetting NFL owners. When something blows up, the owners demand to speak directly with our CEO, and get put straight through. Our CEO says nothing but 'yes sir, yes sir.' We know when the next rights deals are up for grabs, any network that has not appeased NFL ownership runs the risk of being cut out of the action. Basically, we are neutered."

The NFL entered 2015 with contractual relationships with communications conglomerates CBS, Comcast/NBC, DirecTV, Disney/ABC/ESPN, Fox, Hearst, Verizon and Yahoo. Midway through 2015, the league scored another powerful connection when federal regulators allowed AT&T, one of the world's largest communications companies, to purchase DirecTV and assume its monopoly over NFL Sunday Ticket. The league has indirect relationships with Charter Communications, Cox Communications, Time Warner and Viacom, whose cable net-

---

* "The NFL's attitude about concussions is callous and backward."—me on ESPN.com, in 2009.

works realize substantial added value from offering retransmission of NFL games. Seemingly independent Web sites often have corporate links back to the NFL. Bleacher Report is owned by Time Warner; Comcast owns a chunk of Vox Media, which runs SB Nation.

If ABC, AT&T, CBS, Charter Communications, Comcast, Cox Communications, Disney, ESPN, Fox, Hearst, NBC, Time Warner, Viacom, Verizon and Yahoo all are "basically neutered" by a desire to please the billionaires atop the NFL, sports commentary will become even more banal, and sports promotion even more brazen, while the questionable aspects of the NFL are kept far from sunlight.

This disturbing trend is balanced by the continuing tremendous quality of NFL play. The games are really great, and ever-easy to follow as stats and highlights are everywhere. Think the NFL is already too big? Brace yourself.

# 5

# Hey, That's Me in the
# NFL Mirror

The same NFL season that concluded with the trifling PSI-cheated scandal began with an all-too-serious controversy: the Ray Rice video.

In February 2014, Rice, a star performer for the Baltimore Ravens—he was the team's leading rusher in its Super Bowl victory over San Francisco—punched his fiancée, Janay Palmer, knocking her unconscious. The incident occurred in an elevator at Revel Atlantic City, a shiny-new glass-and-chrome obelisk along the Atlantic City boardwalk. The complex boasted fourteen hundred hotel rooms, poker, blackjack, roulette and many other casino games, three dining rooms and a twenty-four-hour Asian noodle bar themed as a streetscape in Roppongi, the nightlife district of Tokyo. Struggling to gain recognition at a time of rising online gambling, the casino offered to "comp" boldface names from athletics and entertainment. It was good business for celebrities to be seen strolling through the lobby or having noodles at 3 a.m. Because the Revel Atlantic City was brand new, there were security cameras practically everywhere, including in elevators.

THE GAME'S NOT OVER

Observing a struggle, casino security summoned police. Initially Rice and Palmer both were charged with assault—responding officers believed Palmer started the fight. In March 2014, Rice was indicted for aggravated assault while charges against Palmer were dropped. After the indictment, Rice and Palmer married. She would say she forgave him, and strongly dispute that her decision resulted from battered-woman syndrome.

Because Rice had a clean record, prosecutors allowed him to enter a pretrial diversion program of counseling and supervision: in exchange, remaining charges were dropped. A substantial body of criminology supports leniency for first offenders who show remorse. Roger Goodell suspended Rice for the initial two contests of the coming autumn season, calling this the maximum bad-conduct penalty, under the league's collective bargaining agreement with its union, for a player not convicted of a crime. At that juncture the NFL hoped the matter was closed.

Later, Goodell would contend he had no way of knowing the incident was violent or that there was a videotape. Yet, one day after the fight, the *Newark Star Ledger* reported, "Ravens running back Ray Rice knocked his fiancée, Janay Palmer, unconscious during an altercation in Atlantic City early Saturday morning." Roundhouse punches are violent—what part of "unconscious" did Goodell not understand? And in March 2014, CBS Sports reported, "Security footage from the night of incident shows Rice dragging Palmer out of an elevator at Revel Casino. Palmer appears to be unconscious and doesn't move at any point during the 51-second video."

On September 2, 2014, just before opening day of the new NFL season, the Revel Atlantic City closed, done in by a gambling industry that had too many glittering casinos chasing not enough marks. Someone from the hotel's security office, now jobless and beyond the scope of a boss's retaliation, sold the elevator video to an organization future anthropologists will have no hope of understanding—the beautiful-people gotcha show, TMZ.

On September 8, TMZ aired the video. America beheld grainy images of an NFL star assaulting a woman. Aiming to make the story go viral, TMZ digitally manipulated the image to give the impression Rice struck Palmer over and over, rather than once.

Reaction to the video of Ray Rice punching his fiancée was a national gasp. Within hours, the Ravens waived Rice. Cable news, talk radio and social media spoke of little else. Women's groups demanded Rice be barred from the NFL. Goodell suspended him indefinitely, though previously had claimed to lack this authority.

Many NFL players denounce the commissioner for disciplinary actions: after being suspended for a vicious hit to an opponent's face, Pro Bowl linebacker James Harrison called Goodell "the devil." The commissioner hands out fines, owners hand out paychecks—so players like the owners and dislike Goodell.

Players contend that standards for conduct penalties are inconsistent. When Harrison punched an opponent in the face in the 2009 Super Bowl, there were no consequences; when he hit an opponent in the face in 2011, suspension followed. The difference was that the sports press missed the former foul but called attention to the latter. The bottom line is that the commissioner penalizes players not for being unethical, but for causing bad publicity. Because the bad publicity, not the behavior, is treated by the league front office as the offense, punishments are all over the map: there's no predicting why pack journalism ignores one event and then is hysterical over a similar event. Initially, Rice's behavior caused the NFL only a moderate amount of bad publicity, so punishment was moderate. Once the video was out, bad publicity was rampant: Rice's goose was cooked.[*]

A mere six weeks had passed from when Goodell thought he'd washed his hands of Rice, with minimal harm to "the shield"—league insiders speak of the NFL's logo and its reputation as synonymous—to a four-alarm panic.[†] Ours is a visual society, so the video carried an impact words never could: though what was shown was no different from what had been known factually for months. Actually seeing the punch rendered fairly obvious that the NFL and the Baltimore Ravens,

---

[*] The same sequence played out in PSIcheated. When Tom Brady was causing only moderate bad publicity, little action was taken. Once (fairly or not) his actions caused a bad publicity avalanche, it was Katy bar the door, whatever that means.

[†] By 2015, the NFL had become so sensitive to public criticism that the Atlanta Falcons immediately waived a player named Prince Shembo when he was charged with cruelty to animals for killing a dog. Later the charge was dismissed, when it was shown the dog first bit Shembo: yet the Falcons did not want their player back. Whether employees should be fired merely for being arrested—that is, before any accusation is proven—is a troubling question. But the Ray Rice experience caused the NFL to veer from doing too little to overreaction.

owned by the publicly subsidized billionaire Steve Bisciotti, had engaged in a clumsy cover-up attempt.

The commissioner gave a series of contradictory explanations for his actions. A dispute began regarding whether Goodell had seen the video before imposing the original two-game suspension. Former FBI Director Robert Mueller was hired to get to the bottom of that wearying question. The report Mueller produced was intended to be a whitewash, its docile tone entirely different from the harsh PSIcheated report the league would commission a few months later. Mueller pocketed a nice fee for producing a document preordained to vindicate NFL senior management: every owner had an interest in the Sargent Schultz conclusion.[*] The later report on football inflation made only the Patriots look bad—an outcome many owners desired.

At a press conference on the Rice video, every question was hostile, Goodell visibly squirming. Even Judy Battista, one of the commissioner's employees—she works for NFL.com, "Official Site of the National Football League"—was openly antagonistic to Goodell, then followed up with a piece on NFL.com calling the league's domestic-violence policies "badly broken." Just two years after being depicted on the cover of *Time* magazine as a man of power and vision, Goodell was subjected to wide ridicule.

Typically when big organizations are in trouble they make a public-relations gesture, and the NFL did. The league promoted an official in its community-affairs department to a new position, NFL Vice President of Social Responsibility. Exactly what

---

[*] "I see nothing, nothing!"

Anna Isaacson, bearer of this exalted title, does is unclear, other than provide a female face on issues of domestic violence and sexual assault. Big organizations in trouble also typically make donations to charity: in the wake of the video, the NFL gave $25 million to the National Domestic Violence Hotline, a counseling service.

Donations and PR gestures did not prevent the public stature of the NFL from declining. This was another of the many ways in which the NFL holds up a mirror to society. Respect for institutions is decaying. Business, the Pentagon, the media, religious denominations are all losing stature. Polling data in 2015 showed that only 9 percent of Americans approved of the job Congress is doing, which raised the question: Who on earth are those crackpot 9 percent? In years past, the NFL could stonewall criticism by telling the public what to believe. The Rice controversy showed that the days of telling the public what to believe are over.

Lost in the shuffle was whether Rice's original punishment, the two-game suspension, had been sufficient for a first-time offender whose victim made a bona fide decision to forgive.* Rice wasn't the sole NFL player accused of domestic violence in 2014. Carolina Panthers Pro Bowl player Greg Hardy was arrested for assault against his girlfriend, 2012 MVP Adrian Pe-

---

* Ultimately Rice did not play in 2014, reaching a confidential settlement with the Ravens that is believed to have paid him most of what he would have earned on the field. At this writing, Rice had been cleared to return to the NFL but no team had offered him a roster spot, fearing demonstrations at games. Janay Rice's question about the whole matter—"Why can't I be the one who makes the decision about how I lead my life?"—had been pushed aside.

terson was accused of child abuse, and police were called more than once to the home of 49ers star Ray McDonald to respond to domestic violence complaints.* These cases pushed several issues to the forefront of public debate. Among them was whether football players are more violent than men as a whole; whether police avert their eyes from crimes by NFL players; whether there exists a relationship between football and abuse of domestic partners.

Multiple NFL players accused of domestic violence created an impression that such behavior was endemic to the testosterone-pumped reality of the NFL. Or perhaps the reason for the intensity of the Ray Rice controversy was that it symbolized what many men from all walks of life were doing to many women.

One of the limitations of crime statistics is that arrests are more closely tracked than the dispositions (conviction, acquittal or charges dropped) of cases. As regards the former, *USA Today* keeps a database of arrests of NFL players. The *USA Today* numbers show that slightly more than one NFL player in fifty—about 2 percent of NFL players overall—is arrested in any given year.

How does this compare to men as a group? In the most recent census year, 2010, there were 115 million U.S. adult

---

* Hardy settled out of court with his accuser, in return for her not pressing charges; at this writing, he had joined the Dallas Cowboys and was suspended for the first four games of 2015. Peterson pleaded no contest to a misdemeanor and, at this writing, had rejoined the Minnesota Vikings for the 2015 season. McDonald, several times accused but, at this writing, never convicted of any violent crime, was signed by the Bears, then promptly waived after he was arrested again.

males. The Justice Department's Bureau of Justice Statistics reports that 8.6 million of them were arrested. That's 7.5 percent of American adult men being arrested in a year. The share is surprisingly large, one man in thirteen arrested. It may suggest, as some believe, that the United States has too many laws and too many people thrown into jail for what ought to be handled as citations.* The number also shows that NFL players are significantly less likely to be arrested than adult American men overall.

On September 5, 2014, just a few days before the Rice video aired on TMZ, the Centers for Disease Control released a detailed meta-study of the hauntingly named "intimate violence." The report found that physical harm inflicted by a domestic partner—what Ray Rice did—is experienced by 2.3 percent of American women and 2.1 percent of American men in a given year; by 22.3 percent of American women and 14 percent of American men during a lifetime.† This study drew just shy of zero attention. A few days later, the entire country was talking about the NFL star who clocked his fiancée.

Domestic violence in the National Football League held up a mirror to a society trying to come to grips with how often such crimes occur, whether those responsible (usually but not always men) belong in jail or in counseling, and whether the victims (usually but not always women) should go public. The

---

* See the book *One Nation Under Arrest* by Paul Rosenzwieg.

† While domestic violence surely is underreported, prosecution is more likely than assumed. Researchers Joel Garner and Christopher Maxwell showed in a 2008 study in *Criminal Justice Review* that about one-half of domestic violence reports filed with police result in a criminal conviction.

numbers in the CDC study show that "intimate" violence is far more prevalent than anyone would care to believe—certainly, than has been acknowledged in public debate. Domestic abuse in an average family has exactly the same moral and legal importance as domestic abuse in the family of an NFL star. But because the latter is what's noticed, the stark realization that NFL players whip their young children (Peterson) or beat up their girlfriends (Hardy) brought into the light things that happened in families whose names we don't know.*

NFL players may be less likely to commit crimes than men as a whole, but when an NFL player commits an illegal act, the nation notices. Football players at the pro, college and even high school levels complain they are called to account for transgressions, like traffic tickets and having too much to drink, that in other circumstances would be viewed as insignificant. But football players not only enjoy extensive privileges, they hold society's mirror. Sometimes when we see the bad they do, what we are really seeing is the bad society does.†

---

* Hardy was found guilty of assaulting his girlfriend and appealed; when the girlfriend settled with him out of court, then did not appear at a hearing required by North Carolina law, the original charge against Hardy was dropped. So what's the fair way to describe his legal situation? Since signing Hardy in 2015, the Dallas Cowboys have struggled with that question.

† Rice, Peterson, and Hardy were all banished from the league for at least a year, genuine penance considering how short NFL "careers" are. By contrast, when NFL owners admit wrongdoing, there are few consequences. In 2014, Indianapolis Colts owner James Irsay pleaded guilty to driving while intoxicated with oxycodone and hydrocodone. The NFL fined Irsay $500,000, about 2 percent of the Colts' annual operating profit and about 0.1 percent of public subsidies to Lucas Oil Stadium, from which Irsay keeps nearly all football revenue. Workers punished, owners not punished—another reflection of American life writ large.

The intensity of the reaction to the Ray Rice situation suggests the country was using the NFL to shed taboos regarding discussion of domestic violence. Most people can't bear the thought that their neighbors, friends, coworkers or family members harm their spouses or lovers, but can bear the thought of NFL players engaged in such acts. And if those living the good life of wealth and celebrity in the nation's highest-profile sports organization get wrapped up in this problem, couldn't anyone? A newspaper series on domestic violence statistics might never make that point in the way the NFL elevator video did. Nor lead to the conclusion that if bringing the problem into the light of day is best for the families of NFL stars, maybe this is best for everyone.

Another example of the nation working through taboos by using the NFL reflection is the 2013 Miami Dolphins bullying scandal. Jonathan Martin, an offensive lineman for the Dolphins—a recent high draft selection and starter at the all-important left tackle slot—quit the team, saying he'd been bullied in the locker room. Martin declared he experienced "emotional distress" caused by bullying. As an example, he said other offensive linemen waved to him to join them at the lunch table, then when he happily sat down, they all got up with their trays and walked away laughing.

That sort of mean trick might cause any nine-year-old to burst into tears. But Martin is a 315-pound football star who can bench-press a railroad locomotive. The thought that a huge, brawny athlete could suffer emotional pain would have been scoffed at not just by the previous generation of NFL coaches, but by the prior generation of sportswriters. Some columnist would have spun out a piece telling Martin he'd better man up—take the leader of the bullies outside and show him who's boss. Any football player who complains about bullying by teammates is a wimp! Answer them with your fists!

Instead, there was national fixation on the NFL bullying scandal, with sentiment on Martin's side. This reflected the evolving sense in American society that bullying is not just bad manners but unethical, even criminal. And if someone with fantastic biceps can be bullied, can't anyone?

The growth of social media was making bullying easier. Those who bully in person expose themselves to a risk the target will answer with fists; any coward can bully from the shadows using a computer or smartphone. But by the same token, digital bullying creates records. Prior generation accusations of bullying were one person's word against another's. Social-network bullying leaves a transcript.

Around the time of the Martin situation, the public learned of several heartbreaking stories of tween or teen girls, or gay young boys, committing suicide after being bullied. In a few instances criminal charges were filed against peers, or adults, who did the bullying.[*] To prior generations, bullying was just a fact of life—you had to learn to deal with it. Now a national consensus was forming that bullying should not be a fact of life; that bullies should at the least be shunned, perhaps punished by the legal system.

Suddenly the National Football League was offering a morality play on exactly this topic, including obsessive dissection

---

[*] The facts and legal aspects of such cases are analyzed in the terrific 2013 book *Sticks and Stones* by Emily Bazelon.

of hundreds of text messages and voice mails exchanged by Martin and his tormenter, a teammate named—and this is his real name—Richie Incognito. The NFL commissioned what grew into a 144-page report, anticipating the even-longer report that would follow on underinflated footballs.* Incognito appeared on Fox Sports to present a long mea culpa, acknowledging he'd filled text messages to Martin with racist slurs and indecent language but contending this is standard locker-room talk. (It is, which is part of the problem.) A week after the controversy began, the Dolphins suspended Incognito for the remainder of the season. No team wanted him for the season that followed, though he's a good blocker, and in the NFL, good blockers are always in short supply.†

That the NFL, America's citadel of machismo, did not want to be seen as tolerating bullying is a sign of changing social values—something once swept under the rug now viewed as shameful. Perhaps the strongest indicator of this transition was ESPN's *Sunday NFL Countdown* show of the week the Martin story broke. This talkfest features former NFL stars Keyshawn Johnson and Cris Carter yakking it up with the ultimate tough guy, former Chicago Bears player and coach Mike Ditka. One would have expected *Sunday NFL Countdown* to make small of Martin's situation: for Ditka to say, "When I was coaching, if some fruitcake had come into my office whining that the other guys weren't being nice to him...."

---

* Both reports were overseen by lawyer Ted Wells, who has developed a really specialized practice—NFL public-relations tsunamis.

† Incognito began the 2015 season with the Buffalo Bills and by all accounts was minding his Ps and Qs, whatever that means.

Instead, the vibe of the show was subdued, almost funereal. Carter, Johnson and Ditka agreed the Dolphins players who bullied Martin should be ashamed of themselves. They took turns declaring that racial slurs and cruel behavior had no place in any athletic locker room. It wasn't so much that football was changing, rather that the country was changing, and football was reflecting the new reality. Towel-snapping frat-boy behavior, boorish comments about women and gays—things once common in the workplace—increasingly are viewed as demeaning to everyone, including to straight men. And the football locker room is, after all, a workplace.

Nowhere were evolving American social views better seen than when University of Missouri defensive end Michael Sam came out as gay shortly before the 2014 NFL draft. Sam was a collegiate star: many (certainly not all) touts expected him to make an NFL roster.[*] Sam was the first potential NFL player to present himself as openly gay. When he was chosen late in the draft by the St. Louis Rams, not just CNN but the NFL Network showed him kissing his boyfriend in celebration.

If the Ray Rice video caused a national gasp, Michael Sam caused something akin to an earth tremor. An openly gay football star seemed a step in the direction of honesty and acceptance. But some were shocked. New Orleans Saints linebacker

---

[*] Shortly after Sam made his announcement, yours truly noted on ESPN that five years earlier a player at the same position in the same conference with very similar college stats and combine numbers to Sam, Antonio Coleman of Auburn, never made an NFL gameday roster. When Sam did not make the NFL either, some claimed anti-gay bias. The league is so competitive, many college stars never suit up in the NFL.

Jonathan Vilma declared he would not want to shower with a gay teammate.

The likelihood is that Vilma has taken many showers with homosexual teammates, just not known it. A gay man has the same chance as any man of being musclebound and macho, just as a lesbian has the same chance as any woman of being pretty and feminine. The Williams Institute at UCLA, a leading academic source for data on the LGBT community, estimates 1.7 percent of American adults are gay or lesbian, and that another 1.8 percent are bisexual. That suggests there are around thirty gay players in the NFL, and around ten lesbian NFL cheerleaders, along with another forty-five NFL players and cheerleaders who are bisexual.[*]

Ultimately, Michael Sam would bounce around the taxi squads of the Rams and Cowboys, then land with the Montreal Alouettes of the Canadian Football League. When Sam appeared in NFL preseason contests, crowd reaction was positive. There's no indication he experienced any NFL backlash against his sexuality—merely joined countless collegiate stars in lacking the extra gear needed in a super-competitive league. That Sam's Rams jersey was among the high-demand sports apparel items of 2014, outselling the jerseys of established NFL names Drew Brees and Aaron Rodgers, is an indicator of broad social acceptance for the first openly gay performer in NFL pads.

Within a year after Sam's coming out, thirty-six states had legalized marriage independent of gender, and then the Supreme Court made the concept universal. On the day of the

---

[*] It seems only a matter of when, not if, the first NFL cheerleader comes out. This may already have happened by the time you read this book.

June 2015 Supreme Court decision, polls showed a majority of Americans supported civil recognition of gay marriage—including a substantial fraction of Republicans and, most tellingly, 70 percent of millennials.

When president, Bill Clinton opposed gay unions: he backed and signed the 1996 Defense of Marriage Act, whose primary title defined marriage as between a man and a woman. Clinton always had his finger in the wind: in 1996, just 27 percent of Americans supported same-gender nuptials. In 2008, Barack Obama ran for the White House as opposing gay marriage, surely because polls showed a strong political consensus against the idea. By 2012, Obama said his views had "evolved"—maybe this really happened, but more likely Obama saw poll numbers showing the nation's views had evolved. America's 180-degree change, from little tolerance of gayness in the 1990s to strong support for gay marriage twenty years later, in 2015 was called by the *Wall Street Journal* "the most dramatic cultural shift in U.S. history." One of the leading indicators of that shift was that the National Football League accepted a gay player.

Domestic violence, bullying, sexual orientation—none seem to possess any direct connection to professional football, and traditionalists of prior generations would have been appalled to think the NFL should become involved with such issues. Yet the nation was trying to come to terms with all three, and projected its feelings onto America's national sport.

**Postscript:** though the NFL has made halting progress regarding violence against women, the league has a very long way to go.

NFL star O.J. Simpson, at this writing serving a prison sentence for armed robbery, in 1989 pleaded no contest to assaulting his wife Nicole Brown. In 1992, Brown and Simpson divorced. Two years later Brown was savagely murdered in the doorway of her home, her throat cut so deeply she was nearly decapitated. A friend named Ronald Goldman was stabbed to death while attempting to defend her. Following a long, strange trial, Simpson was acquitted of criminal charges in the murders. In 1997, a California civil jury found Simpson liable for both deaths.

Yet O.J. Simpson's bust is still in the Pro Football Hall of Fame in Canton. His face still adorns an exhibit, his records still are lauded—not a word said about his assault against his wife or her slit throat.* Parents taking their kids to see exhibits of football history in Canton can take them to the Simpson exhibit, where the topic of violence against women magically disappears.

Equally bad, Simpson's name stains the Wall of Fame at Ralph Wilson Stadium in Orchard Park, New York, a publicly owned facility that in 2014 received $130 million in state taxpayers' money, financing upgrades to make the stadium more profitable for the NFL. Parents taking their kids to watch the Buffalo Bills in a publicly subsidized facility see a name associated with the sadistic murder of a woman, displayed as that of someone

* Technically the NFL does not control the Hall of Fame, but that's like saying technically the White House has no influence over the Federal Reserve. If the NFL cared one hoot about Simpson's name in Canton or on the wall of a publicly subsidized NFL stadium, this would change. And the Hall of Fame has not-for-profit status, meaning taxpayers grant a major favor to a facility that pretends there's no such thing as violence against women.

heroic to be admired. Women attending games at Ralph Wilson Stadium see a violent misogynist acclaimed at taxpayer expense. Great football players who behaved with honor—Andre Reed, Billy Shaw, Bruce Smith—have their names on the Wilson Stadium wall. So does a repulsive criminal.

It is clear from the Ray Rice situation that the NFL cares about bad publicity caused by violence against women. Does the league care about the underlying problem? If the National Football League really cared, Simpson's name would long since be gone from the Hall of Fame and the wall of the Bills' stadium.

# Where Barack Obama Was Wrong About the NFL

Twice during his presidency, Barack Obama, an avid foot-ball fan—do you really need more proof Obama is Amer-ican through-and-through?—sat down with intellectuals to discuss the NFL.

In January 2013, the president told Franklin Foer, then edi-tor of the New Republic,* "If I had a son, I'd have to think long and hard before I let him play football." That was the head-line-maker from the interview. Talk radio and cable news sug-gested the comment meant Obama was opposed to the nation's most popular sport.

In the 2013 interview, the president continued: "I tend to be more worried about college players than NFL players in the sense that the NFL players have a union, they're grown men, they can make some of these decisions on their own, and most

---

* Among his many achievements, Foer coedited a book called *Jewish Jocks*, refuting the stereotype that Jews can't be athletes. In the 1980 farce *Airplane*, a passenger asks the flight attendant for something short to read. She hands him a book titled *Famous Jewish Sports Legends*.

of them are well-compensated for the violence they do to their bodies. You read some of these stories about college players who undergo some of these same problems with concussions and so forth and then have nothing to fall back on."

In 2014, Obama again found himself talking football to an intellectual, this time David Remnick, editor of the *New Yorker*. Remnick had been invited aboard Air Force One, where the president was using some kind of space-relayed NSA-caliber electronics to watch the NFL's Panthers and Dolphins. The game was a woofer, Miami fielding a weak squad that season. A few hours later the 9-1 Broncos would face the 7-3 Patriots. New England fell behind 0-24, then came back to win in over-time. If you didn't enjoy that contest, then you don't like sports. By the time the fabulous game began, the president was speaking at a fundraiser.[*]

Obama told Remnick, "I would not let my son play pro foot-ball." Then the chief executive continued, "There's a little bit of caveat emptor. These guys, they know what they're doing. They know what they're buying into. It is no longer a secret. It's sort of the feeling I have about smokers, you know?"

Of course, presidential statements are overanalyzed. Never-theless, consider Obama's second bite of the apple regarding football.

The president, who has two daughters, declares he would not let "my son" play in the NFL. Since Obama has no son, the state-

---

[*] The president, Remnick reports, "was headed for a three-day fundraising trip to Seattle, San Francisco and Los Angeles." That top elected officials of both parties shirk their duties to fundraise at public expense is among the core problems of U.S. politics.

ment is pure conjecture—a little like saying, "Well if I'd been there at Omaha Beach, I would have taken out that pillbox." Lots of people do have sons: if Obama really thinks people's sons should not play in the NFL, he should advocate outlawing professional football. Then again, if Obama did have a son, that child would reach twenty years of age before the NFL would allow him to try out. All NFL players are adults who do not need a parent's permission to assume risks. For these reasons, Obama's "I would not let my son play pro football" rings hollow, even by the low standards of political discourse.

Now compare the rest of the two quotations. In the 2013 interview, the president said he would be hesitant to allow a son play football, period—youth, high school, college or NFL—then expressed concern about concussions at the college level. In the 2014 interview, Obama talked solely of the pros, where "these guys, they know what they're doing." Playing in the NFL, the president suggested, is like lighting up a Marlboro. Everybody knows it's dangerous. If something goes wrong, don't come cryin' about how you weren't warned.

So the first time Barack Obama talked about football risks, he expressed concern for the larger universe of players, almost all of whom never receive an NFL paycheck. The remarks seemed to challenge the ethical standing of football, even its legality, and exposed Obama to several forms of criticism. The president, an immensely skilled politician, realized this, so the second time he talked about football risks, Obama confined himself to the NFL, where players are adults who are highly compensated for their health gamble. Obama changed the conversation from "Are there ethical problems with football as a sport?" to "Is it okay to watch the NFL?" These are entirely distinct questions.

President Obama was correct to say that NFL players "know what they're buying into." The deal such men are offered is an attractive one. Data collected by the NFL Players Association, the pro football union, show that each season roughly one NFL athlete in eight sustains a concussion. Considering players average $2.4 million per year in pay, suppose an employment application said, "Would you accept a one-in-eight chance of a concussion in return for $2.4 million per year?" Most adults would sign that bottom line.

But in the second interview, the president's larger point was far off target. Though no one wants NFL players to be harmed, NFL players should not be the focus of concern. In any given year, there are only about two thousand NFL players, versus about fifty thousand football players at the college level, about 1.1 million in high school,* and around two million players in youth tackle. Almost all neurological harm caused by football occurs below the professional level.

In one sense, this is reassuring to the country's many millions of NFL fans. The question asked in the preface—Is it okay to like pro football?—easily is answered in the affirmative.

Yes, keep watching the NFL. The games are fabulous; the players know the risks and are well compensated. I watch the NFL on television avidly, and attend many games with enthusiasm. I never feel the slightest compunction. You shouldn't either.

---

* This number included a record 1,715 girls playing prep football in 2014, according to the annual survey conducted by the National Federation of High Schools.

A generation ago, when neurological hazards from helmet-to-helmet impacts were hushed up and when football culture encouraged players whose heads hurt to say nothing and return to the field—then, there should have been ethical qualms about watching the NFL. No more. Rising awareness of concussion dangers and of chronic traumatic encephalopathy (CTE), the long-term degenerative brain condition that may be caused by head impacts; rule changes to reduce helmet-to-helmet hits; protocol changes that improve the likelihood concussed players won't go back onto the field;[*] all these things equate to a big thumbs-up for enjoying NFL action. Watch away, without regrets.

Probably you've seen reports of former NFL stars from prior generations who, now passing through late middle age, exhibit dementia, chronic depression, or other neurological issues. Personal stories of mental decline suffered by past-generation NFL players can be harrowing: Hall of Fame star Junior Seau was struggling with depression when he killed himself in 2012.[†]

---

[*] About five years ago, progressive high school and college coaches began taking away the helmets of players with concussion symptoms, so they could not return to the field. The sideline command "Take his helmet!" is a positive sign.

[†] Because full understanding of a suicide often dies with the person, it's impossible to know whether football was a factor in Seau's awful choice. Recently he had divorced, a suicide risk factor, and Seau was first-generation Samoan-American: the Suicide Prevention Resource Center reports that Pacific Islanders are more likely than those from other cultures to experience a sense of shame regarding mental health problems, and not seek help. A 2012 Centers for Disease Control study found that former football players on the whole are less likely to kill themselves than men of the same age. Media commentators who asserted or implied that Seau must have committed suicide because of football—this is like saying, "Kurt Cobain said he took a lot of LSD, so drugs must have caused him to commit suicide."

A 2015 study in the technical journal *Neurology* found retired NFL players from ages forty to sixty-nine were much more likely than other males their age to suffer "cognitive impairment." The study group began playing youth tackle in the late 1950s, the last member leaving the NFL in 1996. Players in that period practiced and performed under brutal conditions, with helmet-to-helmet contact encouraged by coaches; back when there was stigma attached to complaining of head pain; back when coaches rewarded "headhunters," meaning tacklers who led with their helmets.

Today's NFL players have a different experience—fewer knockout-style hits, better neurological care, less live tackling in practice. Only conjecture is possible, but a good guess is that as today's NFL players reach late middle age, they will face fewer brain problems than prior generations. That's another reason viewers can enjoy the NFL without qualms.

But when the lens is focused on the larger football universe, the perspective changes dramatically. Skilled politician Obama shifted the conversation from a troubling topic to one that favors the status quo. The economics of the NFL are broken—Chapter eight will delve into that. But in terms of ethics and social impact, almost all that's troubling about football happens at the youth, prep and college levels.

That one-in-eight NFL concussion annual risk works out to 12.5 percent. How do other levels of the sport compare? The hitting may not be as hard yet concussion risk differs little.

In a 2015 paper in the technical journal *JAMA Pediatrics*, researchers led by Thomas Dompier of Datalys Center for Sports Injury Research and Prevention found that about 10 percent of high school football players sustain a concussion each season, about 5.5 percent of NCAA players, and about 3 percent of youth players.

The National High School Sports Related Injury Surveillance Study, run by Dawn Comstock, a professor of public health at the University of Colorado in Denver, comes to a starker conclusion. In the 2013 football season, the most recent year for which data are available, there were about 148,000 concussions in high school play—a one-in-seven annual chance of concussion, worse than in the NFL. Despite the ferocity of NFL collisions, the pros may be at slightly lower brain injury risk than prep players because professionals are better conditioned, their braincases and neck muscles have finished maturing, and they receive daily medical attention.

Findings regarding neurological harm below the professional level add up to startling totals: 148,000 high school concussions and 60,000 youth concussions. Some 210,000 American boys sustain brain harm annually from football.* That's more than eight hundred football concussions not in the NFL for each one that is. The overwhelming majority of concussions caused by football do not happen to highly paid adults wearing the glorious colors of the National Football League. They happen to youth and high school players—to children.

---

* Research also shows about twenty-five hundred concussions per year in college football, which is about ten times the total for the NFL. While nearly all Division 1 college football players receive full scholarships as compensation for their risk, athletic scholarships are not universal in Division II, and no one receives them in Division III. Since about half of NCAA football occurs at the Division II and Division III levels, a significant fraction of college football concussions are experienced by young men whose play does not pay their tuition.

The next chapter will focus on the implications of the above paragraph. For now let's stay with what is known and not known about brain injuries, and how this factors into public enthusiasm for the NFL versus other levels of the sport.

Very loud noise, falling off a ladder, competitive diving—many circumstances can cause concussions. In June 2015, the *New York Times* sports section led with an article on soccer concussions, which occur with disturbing frequency: including in girls' and women's competition, every bit as rough as boys' and men's matches. Readers who flipped to the next page of the newspaper found a dramatic picture, from the Women's World Cup, of Brazil's Cristiane Rozeira de Souza Silva, face distorted in pain as she slammed her head against an opponent. This picture wasn't part of the soccer-concussion story: rather, accompanied an unrelated article about how World Cup action was so exciting the women were playing through pain to win! *

A Consumer Product Safety Commission study of hospital data from 2009 showed roughly twice as many emergency-room visits for bicycle concussions as for football concussions. Diving and skateboarding combined to result in more emergency-room visits for concussions than did football.

Like many sets of numbers, the ones in this study can be spun. Speaking in 2015 on NFL Network, the league's house channel, Pittsburgh Steelers team neurosurgeon Joseph Maroon

* When Morgan Brian of the United States and Alexandra Popp of Germany dropped to the ground motionless following a violent head-to-head collision during the 2015 Women's World Cup, CBS Sports posted the collision on its Web site *as a highlight.* Football isn't the only sport that needs to get perspective about neurological harm.

declared, "It's much more dangerous riding a bike or a skate-board than playing youth football."

If mortality is the measure, then bicycling is indeed more dangerous. In 2012, the most recent year for which statistics are available, fifteen Americans died because of football[*] while 722 died in bicycle accidents. About two-thirds of the cyclists killed in 2012 were not wearing helmets. If football caused 722 Americans to die in a year, the sport would be outlawed. Yet educators, physicians and community leaders rhapsodize about how wonderful bicycles are, and no one questions the morality of watching the Tour de France.

But the bikes-to-gridiron comparison may not mean, as Dr. Maroon suggests, that football is off the hook. While roughly three million Americans play some version of tackle football annually, some hundred million each year ride a bicycle. Larger numbers for bicycle-caused harm might be expected. Many football concussions do not result in emergency-room visits because victims are examined (whether well or poorly) at the scene. Because biking accidents usually are accompanied by bleeding, emergency-room visits are more probable.

---

[*] Two deaths were caused by injuries sustained during semipro games, where medical care is notoriously poor; thirteen boys and young men on high school and college football teams died during or immediately after practice owing to heat stroke or to hypertrophic cardiomyopathy, a rare heart condition. Heat stroke deaths can be prevented by conscientious coaching. Whether all athletes should be tested for hypertrophic cardiomyopathy is a cost-benefit dilemma. Such testing for all high school athletes would entail spending a great deal of money to prevent a small number of tragic deaths; the same amounts spent in other ways could do more to improve public health. The NFL tests for this condition; so should the big-college athletic programs that wallow in money.

There's another way in which the bicycle-football comparison does not stand up. Injuries caused by bicycle riding are accidents. They're not supposed to happen: no one goes for a bicycle ride expecting to be harmed. Concussions are a normal, integral part of football. Expecting pain is standard for football players.

Life cannot be risk-free: avoiding football hardly ensures no harm. Surely any suburban mother whose boy said, "Mom, I've decided to quit the football team, I'm going to skateboard over to the pool and go diving" would breathe a sigh of relief. Mom can stop worrying about football concussions! That hardly means brain harm risk has been eliminated.

Here once again the country sees its reflection in the NFL. As the taboo of discussing concussions began to fade in recent years, parents, athletes, principals and college administrators have been disturbed by the realization that a range of sports and activities, even cheer, can lead to lasting neurological damage.*
When concussions came out of the closet as an issue of concern, anger centered on NFL indifference. But we were really angry at ourselves. How many youth and high school coaches, how many teachers and physicians and nurses, had seen sports-caused head harm and said nothing? The sense of anger about this focused on our outsized national sport, the NFL absorbing that which should have been directed at society as a whole.

One reason traumatic brain injury from athletics is so trou-

---

* The basket toss—a smiling girl flies upward, does an airborne split, then is caught by other cheerleaders—is great fun to watch and also an injury looking for a place to happen. In 2008, the National Center for Catastrophic Sports Injury Research at the University of North Carolina reported 65 percent of severe athletic injuries to girls and women result from cheerleading and its sister sport, competitive cheer.

bling is that neurology has not advanced as much as orthopedics. Joint pain, torn ligaments and other orthopedic problems in the sort of people who play team sports—the young, who heal quickly—today usually can be corrected through arthroscopy and by drugs that have few side effects. It sucks to tear your ACL or throw out your shoulder, but soon you'll be fine again.

Concussions, by contrast, are very hard to treat. Painkillers can reduce the blinding headaches associated with concussions, but the opioids that do this are addictive. There's no golden-bullet drug for the brain swelling a concussion causes. Brain surgery is expensive, complicated and dangerous compared to inserting an arthroscope into a knee, and in most concussion cases, surgery would not help anyway. Only the passage of time seems to heal. When the prescription for concussion is rest, that may mean doing hardly anything—no sports, no studying, not much more than lying in bed—for weeks. Lying in bed for weeks isn't much fun, and disrupts lives.

Funding has poured into the study of concussions, and so far, results are modest. The *New York Times* reported in July 2015,

> Over the last decade, the Defense Department has spent more than $800 million on brain injury research, with organizations and companies like the National Football League and General Electric spending tens of millions more. As people become aware of the debilitating long-term consequences of repeated concussions, businesses have been chasing salable solutions. Start-ups are marketing their products to the military, schools, hospitals, sports teams and parents, and controversial therapies like hyperbaric oxygen are being

promoted to patients. But as the industry booms, medical experts are raising concerns that it is a business where much of the science is sketchy, belief frequently outruns fact, and claims of technological breakthroughs evaporate soon after they are made.

Until such time as the science of treating brain trauma may improve, neurological harm will be more worrisome than orthopedic harm, because the latter can be corrected and the former often cannot.

Head impacts may lead to CTE, a condition that is poorly understood. Symptoms associated with CTE, such as short-term memory loss, might be brought on by a range of problems that are not CTE. With current science, CTE can be diagnosed in a definitive way only after death. The definitive diagnosis requires a brain autopsy, and such autopsies are rare. And even if a sure test for CTE is devised for the living, there's no known treatment.

It may turn out that many people who never played sports develop CTE because any kind of blow to the head may contribute to this condition. Soldiers and sailors who are around cannons being fired or missiles being launched—thereby exposed to overpressure—are thought to be at risk for CTE, for instance. It may turn out that large numbers of people who've never worn football helmets or been a tank gunner or done anything out of the ordinary nevertheless develop CTE—that the condition is simply a hazard of being alive.

Or it may turn out that football players, ice hockey players, soldiers and a few other categories of people who undergo hard impacts to the head are much more likely to develop CTE than the population as a whole. If a clear link between head impacts and CTE is proven, society may need to reassess its debt to combat veterans—and its enthusiasm for contact sports.

Sued by former players who said the NFL concealed knowledge of how dangerous traumatic brain injuries can be, in early 2015 the league settled with plaintiffs. Assuming the settlement goes into effect—at this writing, there were a few remaining legal hurdles—the NFL will pay around $1 billion over about twenty years as compensation to retired players with dementia, and to fund research.

While $1 billion is not pocket change, the settlement is a sweet deal for the league. After tax deductions, the amount works out to about one-fifth of one percent of the revenue the NFL expects during the settlement period. More important, the settlement was reached before it might be scientifically proven that football causes CTE, and before a way might be found to diagnose CTE in the living. Should either someday happen, the NFL's liability in such a lawsuit would soar. As is, former players accepting compensation must waive any future right to litigate.*

The contention of the former players' lawsuit was that NFL owners, coaches and physicians knew it was unsafe to send concussed athletes back onto the field, but withheld this knowledge from players who, far from being warned, were told they should prove their courage by ignoring brain harm symptoms. Such "asymmetrical information"—one party has

---

* For most, this makes sense. Better some money now than run the risk that years later, at a trial, they lose and get nothing. Tort plaintiffs often face this dilemma.

critical safety information and does not tell the other party—
is a core concept in liability law.

Signing the settlement, the NFL admitted no wrongdoing.
Not admitting guilt was essential from the league's stand-
point—how could states and cities keep awarding subsidies to
an enterprise that admitted decades of deliberate wrongdoing?
But though the NFL confessed nothing, one may safely assume
$1 billion would not have been placed on the table unless the
league knew the former players could prove their claims.

Current NFL players are unlikely to have future grounds to
sue over concussions, since the key information is no longer
asymmetrical. Now everyone's had fair warning.

Some NFL players have taken the warnings to heart. During
the 2015 off-season, the 49ers' Anthony Davis, the eleventh man
chosen in the 2010 draft, retired, saying he wanted to leave before
his "mind and body" were ruined. Chris Borland, the same team's
third-round choice in the 2014 draft, retired after playing a fine
rookie season, citing a desire to avoid concussions. Borland repaid
the 49ers about $465,000 in bonus money in order to walk away
with both a clear head and a clear conscience. Eric Reid, the
49ers' first selection in the 2013 draft, and one of the NFL's top
young performers, disclosed that he had sustained three concussions in his initial two seasons and knew that a fourth concussion
would mean he should stop playing.

These are only a small number of examples. There is hardly
an exodus from the NFL because of neurological risk. Plenty of
young men with fantastic athletic ability are only too happy to
take their chances in the NFL in return for the income and
lifestyle the league offers.

The ending of the taboo regarding concussions has led to many reforms. The rule against deliberate helmet-to-helmet hits, then strict enforcement of that rule. New protocols requiring players with concussion symptoms to be assessed by an independent neurologist, not a team employee. Reduction of contact hours in practice—deceptively important, since football players spend more time in practice than in games. The 2010 decision to move the kickoff spot from the 30 to the 35 increased touchbacks, which reduced kickoff returns, the most concussion-prone play in football.

Beginning with the 2015 season, there is a certified athletic trainer watching each NFL game for signs of players who are trying to remain on the field despite their heads ringing. This new official has authority to pull such players out to be examined. The idea is that a neutral judge will prevent a team that does the right thing regarding players' neurological health from being at a competitive disadvantage to a team that does not.[*]

In the Seattle-New England Super Bowl, Seahawks defensive star Cliff Avril sustained a concussion a few snaps before his team took a 24-14 third quarter lead. Seattle's team doctor ordered Avril out for the remainder of the contest. With Avril off the field, the New England offense came alive, scoring two late touchdowns to win the Lombardi Trophy. During the New

---

[*] The neutral judge of concussions is something my Tuesday Morning Quarterback column has advocated for nearly a decade. If a player breaks his leg, everyone knows; if he sustains a concussion, officials may not be aware and his own coaches may not care. Involving a third party should improve protection of players while preventing the conscientious coach from being at a disadvantage to the win-at-all-costs coach. Once this idea is entrenched at the professional level, it could be extended to college and high school play as well.

England comeback, Patriots wide receiver Julian Edelman took a hard hit to the head. Edelman had missed games two months before because of a concussion; anyone with a recent concussion is at risk of "second impact syndrome." Second-impact concussions are more dangerous, because the brain is already swollen from the first concussion. Yet Patriots coaches did not pull Edelman from the Super Bowl, as Seahawks coaches pulled Avril. Ultimately, Edelman caught the Super Bowl-winning pass. Afterward, he said New England officials had forbidden him to discuss his head injury.

It's impossible to be certain, but seems that Seattle being conscientious, and New England being win-at-all-costs, helped decide the NFL championship. The new neutral judge should prevent such an outcome from repeating. These and other reforms mean NFL players are better safeguarded against traumatic brain injury than a generation ago.

But NFL players are not the ones we should worry about. Like the sitting president, many of us put too much focus on the small number of football professionals. As the next chapter explores, the far larger number below the NFL level should be our concern as regards safety.

Enjoy the spectacular performances of NFL players without reservation. They are well-paid adults exposed to risks that are declining. Nearly every player who makes the NFL will always be glad he did, and we'll always be glad we got to watch. Save your worry power for kids.

|||||||||||||||||||||||||||||||||| **7** ||||||||||||||||||||||||||||||||||

# Is the NFL Bad for Boys
# and Good for Girls?

Suppose logging were a team sport whose pinnacle was the National Logging League. Of course this is fanciful—but during the time of the Founding Fathers, no one would have believed football would happen. So just suppose.

The National Logging League is extremely popular: much of the nation tunes in to watch the Milwaukee Paul Bunyans face the Sacramento Slashfires. There's tension and exciting tactics: teams must prune trees, chop them down, then send their best athletes out to stay atop a log in water during the logrolling competition.* Part of the appeal is the macabre chance to watch a lumberjack killed. Since logging is among America's most hazardous professions—loggers are six times more likely than police officers to suffer occupational death—the NLL sponsors a dangerous sport. But the competitors are well-paid adults who know what they're buying into.

Now suppose millions of boys, and a few girls, grow up

---

* In 2015, the *New York Times* reported that logrolling events have become so popular at state fairs that "logrolling coach" has become a profession.

dreaming of chopping wood in the National Logging League. They participate in youth logging meets where parents get worked up and scream obscenities at the other sideline. Their goal is to make the high school logging team. Lumberjacks are the BMOCs of their schools. Everyone goes to the games, where there are cheerleaders, marching bands, a drum line. On Fridays when the varsity logging team wears plaid flannel shirts and lace-up woodsman boots to class, they're the envy of everyone in the hallway.

The only problem with this arrangement is that high school lumberjacks get into horrifying accidents just like adult lumberjacks. Comparing the adult rate with prep participation, about 1,050 high schoolers would die each year during games. Talk about a downer for Homecoming!

Inevitably, team logging would be outlawed. Even though everyone would agree that the National Logging League was staffed entirely with adults who willingly assumed a risk—just as the United States allows real-world loggers to assume one of society's highest occupational risks—public opinion would conclude that professional team logging was setting a bad example, luring youth and teen players into severe health harm. There aren't many job openings for professional cellists or coloraturas or debaters either, but young people who participate in high school extracurricular activities like these do not jeopardize their long-term well-being. Public opinion would conclude that with only a tiny number of highly paid NLL lumberjack openings to which to aspire, having huge numbers of young people—children—assuming a significant risk in return for almost no chance of finding a career didn't make sense.

The operative difference between the National Football League and the pro logging league of this thought experiment is: chainsaw deaths in competitive logging would be obvious to everyone, whereas brain injury from football cannot be seen by anyone.

Suppose you agree with this book that the ethical issues of football are not at the NFL level, but instead at the youth and high school levels. The really disturbing thing about the ethical issues of football at the youth and high school levels is that the worst-case result, brain trauma, is invisible.

In and of itself, professional football is unobjectionable—grown men who knowingly assume a risk that in their case has an attractive cost-benefit trade-off. But the NFL does not exist in a vacuum. Though schools played the sport before the National Football League attained its postwar popularity, for two generations the national stature of the NFL has driven the expansion and popularity of football below the professional level.

The NFL has a youth affiliate, USA Football, which strives to get little kids into helmets and bashing each other's heads at the youngest possible age. USA Football allows boys (and a few girls) as young as seven to play full-pads tackle. Roger Goodell is on USA Football's board of directors, joined by senior executives from the league and its member franchises. USA Football's corporate partners include Riddell and Sports Authority, which want parents to buy expensive gear for little kids so they can hit each other; CVS, whose MinuteClinic stands by to treat the inevitable injuries; Marriott, where parents can stay while their children are hospitalized; and ESPN, which like the NFL benefits financially from starting fans at an early age.

In 2014, CVS "quit smoking," removing cigarettes from stores. The company wants to be viewed as an advocate of healthful lifestyles. Yet through USA Football, CVS encourages kids as little as seven years of age to get hit on the head.

Here the tobacco analogy applies to the NFL. Cigarettes are a legal product: adults have been warned about them, and may make a free-will choice to smoke. But tobacco companies are forbidden to market to children, because children are impressionable and their bodies are more vulnerable than adults' bodies. Society would be outraged if Philip Morris sponsored junior smokers' clubs where grade schoolers were taught how to light up. With USA Football, the NFL teaches little boys how to light each other up. Because of its active sponsorship of tackle football for the young, the NFL cannot say that youth and high school football is beyond its control.

Now to repeat the paragraph from the previous chapter:

Findings regarding neurological harm below the professional level add up to startling totals: 148,000 high school concussions and 60,000 youth concussions. Some 210,000 American boys sustain brain harm annually from football. That's more than 800 football concussions not in the NFL for each one that is. The overwhelming majority of concussions caused by football do not happen to highly paid adults wearing the glorious colors of the National Football League. They happen to youth and high school players—to children.

Some 210,000 American boys and young men sustain brain harm annually from football. In a culture increasingly based on education, this simply cannot be good. This level of harm to boys is unlike any experienced by girls in athletics. Comstock, of the University of Colorado at Denver, finds about three times as many football concussions as girls' soccer concussions at the high school level.

Children look up to professional football players and fantasize about becoming one of their number. Children fantasize about becoming movie stars, ballet dancers and pop music phenoms, too. But pursuing a fantasy of Hollywood glitter—performing in school musicals, working summer stock—or a fantasy of becoming the next Misty Copeland cannot cause lasting neurological damage. A youthful fantasy of NFL stardom engages this risk at three times the rate of a youthful fantasy of being the next Carli Lloyd.

Since almost all football players are male, both the risks of the sport at the youth through college levels, and the fantasy package created by the NFL and enabled by ESPN,* affect boys and young men almost exclusively.

And what a fantasy package! Little boys see NFL athletes being wealthy celebrities for performing in a game that little boys understand. No ten-year-old can visualize the professional worlds of engineering or medicine or business, but every ten-year-old knows how to play football. Teen boys hear NFL athletes lauded by the media, see NFL athletes driving a Porsche accompanied by a hot blonde. What boy wouldn't want that life! Boys who advance to the stage of college football players see the

---

* Also by AT&T, CBS, Fox, NBC, Verizon and Yahoo—but ESPN is the 365/24/7 enabler.

pros, and that big bonus check, as just one step away. If I get that check, I am set!

The NFL's alluring fantasy package inveigles little boys to put on helmets and sustain brain injuries; teen boys, to ignore their homework chasing the improbable dream of an NCAA football scholarship; NCAA football players, to ignore their classwork chasing the improbable dream of NFL paychecks.

Plenty of girls are football fans, but NFL fantasies do not dance in girls' minds or sidetrack them from homework and classwork. Plenty of girls and young women participate in team sports. But the one they don't participate in, football, is the one causing the most brain injuries and the most schoolwork distractions. Parents rightly complain that club soccer has become a year-round distraction for girls, though only a tiny number will convert athletic prowess into a college scholarship. But simply by squad size, far more high school boys are sidetracked from schoolwork by football than girls are by any sport: especially with nearly all states allowing year-round football meetings and 7 on 7.

Roll together two facts: that almost all football-caused neurological harm happens to boys and young men, and that the leading school-sponsored distraction from school is football. Maybe you'd expect the result to be that girls and young women would be doing better in school than boys and young men. That is exactly the result observed in American society during the period when the NFL has exploded in popularity.

A fundamental of scholarly inquiry is that sociology only infers: premises almost never can be proven.[*] In our case, there

---

[*] Because of this, there is academic debate regarding whether sociology is a science.

is no alternative dimension, in which football does not exist, to use as a control group for the proposition that the gridiron sport's popularity is one cause of boys falling behind girls in the classroom. Thus I concede this chapter presents a lot of speculation. But sometimes, two plus two equals four.

About a generation ago, when the NFL Big Bang occurred—more games, more money, higher ratings, more hype— girls started to outperform boys in high school; women, to outperform men in college. Things happening at the same time do not prove one causes the other. During the period in question, petroleum consumption increased, living standards rose, median household size shrunk—football had nothing to do with these and a hundred other trends that could be named. But there's a case to be made that football did have something to do with educational trends.

According to Department of Education statistics, 1982 was the first year women earned more bachelor's degrees than men. Women's educational achievement began to rise along a steady slope that looks eerily like the slope of rising NFL ratings: plotted against each other on a graph, the lines practically overlap. By the graduating class of 2013, women were awarded 58 percent of bachelor's degrees, 60 percent of master's degrees and 52 percent of doctorates. When associate's degrees are added, Mark Perry, a fellow at the American Enterprise Institute, has noted, today, "140 women graduate with a college degree for every 100 men."

Surely the primary reason is that girls and young women exert themselves more in the classroom than boys and young men do. The secondary reason, in the most recent generation, may be that boys waste more time on video games than do girls.

But rising enthusiasm for football seems a factor too. Large numbers of education-age males injure each other's heads at football, while this happens to almost no education-age females. Playing sports cannot, alone, be the issue, since girls' and women's sports participation has soared during the period when the double-Xs have pulled away from the XYs in education. But almost no double-Xs play tackle football.*

There were about nineteen million high school students in the United States in the 2014-2015 academic year. Of the roughly 1.1 million of them on football teams, all but a handful were boys. That academic year, one high school girl in 8,100 played football, one high school girl in 26 played soccer and one high school boy in 8 played football. The football concussions all went to boys; the I-will-be-an-NFL-star fantasies all were entertained by boys; then the boys did poorly compared to the girls in the classroom.

Because so many high school boys participate in football compared to boys' participation in other extracurriculars, there exists a large cohort of young males daydreaming that football will get them into college. When senior year comes and recruiters do not call, as they almost never do even for prep stars, boys who were daydreaming lack the GPAs and activities for regular admission to college. Surely there are girls who daydream their way through high school too, thinking gymnastics or voice will get them into college, and are in for a rude awakening. And of course many high school kids of both genders simply goof off when they ought to be preparing for college. But the largest

---

* States including Florida now offer high school varsity girls' flag football.

high school cohort that a school-sponsored activity distracts from regular college admission track is boys on the football team. There's no similarly large grouping for girls.

End result? During the same period NFL popularity took off, girls have dominated high school graduation and college admission. "Boys Are No Match for Girls in Completing High School," the *New York Times* story was headlined; "Women's College Enrollment Gains Leave Men Behind," reads the title of the Pew Research Center study. Nationally, 72 percent of girls graduate from high school, compared to 65 percent of boys; of those who receive high school diplomas, 71 percent of girls enroll in college, versus 61 percent of their male counterparts. To the extent such numbers reflect girls and women working harder at education than boys and men, the result is fair-and-square. But to the extent educational gender gaps are impacted by the harm done to boys by football culture, society should be concerned.

The NFL fantasy package may be a factor in the weak graduation rates of African American teens. Today, 80 percent of white high school males graduate, versus 59 percent of black males. At most high schools, blacks are overrepresented on the football team compared to their share of the student body. It may be pleasant for African American tweens and teens to idolize black NFL stars—but an African American male has a more realistic hope of a career in business, government, medicine, law, communications or engineering than in the NFL.

As Harvard University historian Henry Louis Gates, Jr. has noted, there are many times more African Americans in the white-collar professions than in professional sports: about 2,100 black players in the NFL and NBA combined, versus about 270,000 African American engineers, physicians, dentists, lawyers, architects, pharmacists, writers, psychologists and college professors. Gates injured a hip playing football at age fourteen, never recovered his stride, and refocused his energies from sports to education. Probably he had a few months fretting about the gridiron grandeur that was never to be; in retrospect the injury was a stroke of good luck for his future.

For the overwhelming majority of black teens, refocusing from athletics to education is the right course. Any black teen who slights high school classwork as part of a daydream of football stardom is throwing away his chance at the good jobs that outnumber career openings in athletics.

Even at a time of an African American president and African American-run Justice Department, the deck is stacked against young black males in many respects. In contemporary American society, there is one area where the deck is stacked in favor of young black males—college admission.

Today African American males who graduate from high school with good GPAs and board scores are solid gold to college admission offices. Higher education strongly wants black male students, and has a larger pot of regular financial aid to offer than NCAA scholarship money.

So why aren't more African American teens taking advantage? Sports daydreams—especially NFL daydreams, since professional football has more well-to-do black stars than all other U.S. sports combined—sidetrack many black teens from studying. Nobody planned it this way, and obviously sports are hardly the only distraction faced by the young. But the outsized popularity, money, social power and celebrity for NFL players seems to be backfiring on African American tweens and teens, sidetracking them from the classroom. And rightly or wrongly, college, not 40-yard dash times and 225 lift totals, is the gateway to earning power in the United States.

Perhaps the diploma gap between boys and girls is here to stay, and would remain if football magically vanished tomorrow. But there is more than a little chance the sensational success of the NFL is bad for boys and, by reducing the educational competition, good for girls.

The chance of a high school varsity football player reaching the NFL is about one in a thousand. The chance of a high school varsity player both reaching the NFL and remaining for five years—a "career" in NFL terms—is one in four thousand. There simply are too few slots in the NFL to make being a pro football star a realistic ambition.

By contrast, the chance of a college graduate attaining a decent job is only a little below one in one. Earning a bachelor's degree adds $1 million to a male's lifetime earnings; a master's adds $1.5 million.

High school football teaches self-discipline, teamwork, how to organize one's day (a deceptively valuable life skill), the small virtue of being on time, the large virtue of making a commitment and following through. And playing on a high school football team can be a lot of fun. Life goes by so quickly—fun matters.

But if football distracts boys from preparing for college, the costs outweigh the benefits. I played in high school, then at the small-college level; both my sons played in middle school; one went on to varsity football and then was a two-year NCAA starter. Football was fun, and a learning experience, for all of us. But that was because we never lost track of the fact that finishing homework, preparing for the college classroom and doing well there was more important than anything that happens in shoulder pads.

Increasingly, boys lose track of this. The rising prevalence of NFL glory images in culture make the temptation to lose track ever-harder to resist.

Whether young and teen boys can be persuaded to spend more time with books than with sneakers and videogame controllers is a major question facing American society. As we grapple with that question, there's a simple step all parents can take: do not let kids play full-pads tackle until middle school.

Research shows pee-wee football collisions produce disturbingly violent acceleration levels—thirty to fifty times the force of gravity. That's roughly the same impact as Division 1 NCAA hits. Research also shows that until around age thirteen or fourteen, the braincase has not finished hardening and neck muscles are relatively infirm—why little kids are more vulnerable to neurological harm than older teens. Robert Stern, a neurologist at Boston University, has found that aging former football players who began to play tackle before age twelve are much more likely to suffer cognitive decay than those who did not put on pads until they were at least twelve.

I did not let my boys play organized tackle football until middle school. But don't take my word for it: take Archie Manning's. He did not let Peyton and Eli put on pads until seventh grade. Dad being a former NFL star, Archie knew there was no good reason for a youth-league-aged child to take on a brain-injury hazard. Before seventh grade, future Hall of Famers Peyton Manning and Eli Manning were only allowed to play flag.

Parents and guardians, impose the same limit on your children. Flag football provides the enjoyment of pads football with almost no jeopardy to the brain. Flag football teaches kids how to be in the right place at the right time during fluid football action. At age ten, this is a more important lesson than how to hit hard. Parents, encourage your kids to play flag, and don't let them put on helmets until they are at least the age when Peyton and Eli did. If we love football because we idolize its heroes, let's start emulating their smart choices.

# Knocking Pro Football
# Down to Size

During three marvelous spring days in 2015, the National Football League threw itself a party. The NFL took over Chicago's storied lakefront Grant Park, where, in November 2008, just before the clock struck midnight, Barack Obama addressed a vast throng to accept the presidency of the United States. The NFL also took over Chicago's ornate, historic Auditorium Theater, completed in 1889, where John Philip Sousa once conducted a performance of *The Stars and Stripes Forever*.

The 2015 event was the NFL draft. Some two hundred thousand football fans, including many parents with kids, milled around in Grant Park, temporarily renamed Draft Town. Gigantic letters spelling out

N
F
L

ran down the side of the world's largest marble-clad structure, the 83-story Aon Center,[*] an iconic skyscraper designed by Edward Durell Stone.

In Draft Town there were football exhibits; kids could try to catch a machine-thrown pass or kick a field goal. Fans couldn't actually observe players being drafted, much less glimpse NFL commissioner Roger Goodell, who had become to the twenty-first century what viceroys were to previous eras. But they could be near him! Later, they could tell friends and schoolmates, "I was there for the NFL draft."

Players walked across the stage at the gilt-decorated Auditorium Theater, whose entrances were elaborately guarded by police to prevent average fans from entering. Each NFL team had staff present, including the head coach and usually, the owner. ESPN and NFL Network built extravagant sets for their talking heads. Stage crews scurried about, as though for a Broadway opening night. Every number-one choice man-hugged Goodell and declared being very, very happy to be chosen. The throng outside in Grant Park cheered wildly for each draftee, even if they'd never heard of the player. ("With the twenty-first selection of the 2015 NFL draft, the Cincinnati Bengals choose Cedric Ogbuehi, offensive tackle.") During the days of the draft, several downtown streets were blocked. Motorcades raced through the Loop and lakefront areas, NFL officials receiving stopped-traffic police escorts, like visiting heads of state.

---

[*] Opened in 1973 as the Standard Oil Building, the skyscraper is now owned by Aon, a British risk-management firm. Not far away, the even taller skyscraper opened in the same year as the Sears Tower is now the Willis Tower, owned by Willis Group...a British risk-management company.

Both Obama's 2008 acceptance speech and the 2015 NFL draft were huge successes for the civic spirt of the City of Big Shoulders.* Both drew enormous crowds and were nationally televised: both made Chicago seem an exciting, vital place to be. But there was one difference. Obama covered the cost of his event. The NFL was mooching off the taxpayer.

Obama's campaign committee paid Chicago about $2 million as a rental fee to use Grant Park, and to cover police overtime costs for maintaining order. By the moment he stepped to the microphone on November 4, 2008, Obama was president-elect—the third chief executive from Illinois, and like the other two,† bound for the history books. Since Obama was appearing in Grant Park both as a hometown hero and as the first African American president, his acceptance speech engaged a clear public interest. But Obama took the high road, believing it would be unfair for city taxpayers to to be saddled with the expense.

The NFL's billionaire owners preferred the low road, arriving in Chicago with their hands out. Obama, whose reputation is as a spendthrift liberal, covered the costs of his Grant Park appearance. NFL owners, whose reputations are of fire-breathing conservatives extolling self-reliance and the free market, demanded a debt-based giveaway. To the extent life is a hustle, recent history has shown that talking free-market capitalism while lining your pockets with public subsidies is an effective hustle. It's one at which the NFL excels.

---

* This 1916 description from Carl Sandburg is a better nickname than the grating "Chicagoland" that civic promoters use.

† Lincoln, of course; also Ulysses Grant, for whom Grant Park is named.

Negotiating to hold the draft in Chicago, the NFL said it would come only if awarded free use of Grant Park. The city waived the $937,000 fee normally charged for large events there—the sole time, the *Chicago Tribune* reported, a for-profit enterprise received use of Grant Park without a fee. The Auditorium Theater was provided free as well, with taxpayers picking up utility costs for all the lighting and television transmission facilities. The NFL provided no security deposits against damage to either venue. Had damage occurred, taxpayers would have been left on the hook as NFL owners boarded their private jets to depart.

The league's agreement with Chicago specified the city would pay for police overtime, firefighter and ambulance calls, and for any "weather mitigation" necessary, while "the NFL will retain all revenue from tickets and advertising" sold. Chicago gave the NFL the right to close streets in the Loop and along the lakefront, and to remove any signs the league did not like: essentially Chicago suspended the First Amendment, so protestors could not raise banners that mentioned domestic violence, tax subsidies or brain harm. As if the House of Romanov were touring to review the peasants, the NFL demanded free stopped-traffic police escorts "in and around the city" for "certain NFL dignitaries." Certain NFL *dignitaries*.

Public spending on the NFL's self-promotion event was moved off the books by making arrangements through a secretive organization called Choose Chicago. Officially this concern is independent of government, hence not covered by the Illinois Freedom of Information statute. Yet there are many city officials on the board, while 85 percent of Choose Chicago revenues come from city coffers. Both the *Chicago Tribune* (leaning Republican) and

*Chicago Sun-Times* (leaning Democratic) editorialized that NFL draft money was funneled through Choose Chicago as a subterfuge to mask subventions to the rich. For its part, Choose Chicago announced it "planned" to raise private donations to repay the city.

Perhaps Choose Chicago really will raise donations to reimburse the city. But why should this be necessary—why didn't the NFL pay its own way in the first place? The National Football League is a highly profitable private enterprise, with $12 billion in annual revenue. Private enterprise should be self-sufficient. Instead, the NFL's Chicago event was strictly on the dole.

The corporate welfare the NFL received in Chicago is just a small slice of a much larger problem with the league, which is highly subsidized by taxpayers and elaborately protected by government. Here, surely, is another way in which America's biggest sport holds up a mirror to American society: the very rich receive too many publicly funded favors, while celebrities are treated as above the law. Taxpayer support for the NFL draft combined with police escorts for NFL "dignitaries"—dignitaries!—shows both problems.

The league's primary subsidies flow to construction and operation of stadia. All are at least partially publicly funded: some, entirely publicly funded. Judith Grant Long, a professor of sports management at the University of Michigan, estimates that taxpayers provide about 70 percent of the cost of building and operating the fields where NFL teams play. Yet the NFL's owners keep more than 90 percent of revenue generated at their subsidized facilities, while AT&T, CBS, Comcast/NBC, Disney/ESPN, Fox, Verizon and Yahoo profit through transmission of the copyrighted NFL images produced in publicly subsidized stadia.

The NFL is on the dole in numerous other respects. Most of the league's facilities either pay no property taxes (such as Texas's AT&T Stadium, where the Cowboys perform) or are taxed at a far lower rate than comparable local businesses (such as New Jersey's MetLife Stadium, where the Giants and Jets cavort). Stadium construction deals often involve significant gifts of land from the public for NFL use (such as Levi's Stadium in Santa Clara, California, where the "San Francisco" 49ers play).

Hidden costs may include city or county government paying electricity, water and sewer charges for a stadium (such as First Energy Stadium in Cleveland, where the Browns perform), the city paying for a new electronic scoreboard out of "emergency" funds (ditto First Energy) or the issuance of tax-free bonds that divert investors' money away from school, road and mass-transit infrastructure (Hamilton County, Ohio, issued tax-free bonds to fund the stadium where the Cincinnati Bengals play, and has chronic deficits for school and infrastructure needs as a result). And NFL stadiums may have private funding that actually is subsidy disguised by creative bookkeeping. (Some upfront costs for the new facility under construction for the Atlanta Falcons are provided by a hotel tax—but in later years the Falcons' owner, not the city, keeps proceeds from the tax, essentially refunding much of the team's capital expense.*)

---

* Many NFL stadia are funded partly by raising hotel, airport, and rental-car taxes. City and county politicians like such levies because they can be presented to voters as paid by out-of-state travelers, not by local residents. But a rule of neoclassical economics is that whatever you tax, you get less of. Raising taxes on hotels, rental cars, and airports discourages use, depressing local economic activity. This is one of the reasons NFL stadium spending never produces the promised economic multiplier effects.

Wherever the NFL's "dignitaries" tread, they expect taxpayer-funded special treatment. The league's proposal to stage the 2018 Super Bowl at the new publicly-funded Minnesota Vikings stadium in Minneapolis included a demand that NFL owners stay in free presidential suites at the best hotels, that the NFL keep all proceeds from ticket sales and that NFL owners and headquarters officials receive police escorts, at public expense, as they move around the city, including to parties. Supposedly the latter was for "security" against "terrorism." The owners and top executives of the NFL are private business people. If they desire security beyond what is normally accorded in public places by law enforcement, they could pay for it themselves. But the escorts aren't for security, and certainly have nothing to do with terrorism.* The escorts are to allow the limos and SUVs bearing NFL owners, and commissioner Goodell, to speed through traffic, run red lights and cut others off.

The NFL even accepts subsidies for pretending to care about the U.S. military. Flyovers have become a standby: it was the F-16s of the Air Force's Thunderbirds at the most recent Super Bowl. Perhaps flyovers can be rationalized as good publicity for armed services recruiting. Games often are preceded by color guards, or the display of various military banners. This promotes the NFL, not the military, by suggesting professional

---

* The notion that hooded assassins are creeping up behind NFL owners would be rejected by Saturday Night Live writers as too ludicrous for sketch comedy. For the record, George W. Bush's National Commission on Terrorist Attacks Upon the United States concluded that no specific American individual had ever been targeted by terrorists.

football somehow is related to national security.* The NFL stages an annual "Salute to Service" event during Veterans Day weekend, in which coaches dress up in fatigues as if they were military officers, again trying to create the impression the NFL has some relationship to defense of the nation.

At least the league is showing appreciation to service members, right? If only. In 2015, Senator John McCain of Arizona disclosed that the Pentagon pays the NFL about $2 million per year to stage what appear to be displays of patriotism. Included in 2014 was $675,000 to the New England Patriots to honor National Guard members at halftime: most other NFL teams received payments for introducing color guards, and for similar bunting-dressed activities. The billionaire owners in their subsidized stadia expect to get taxpayers' money for creating the appearance that they are thanking the troops. As for that "Salute to Service," in 2014 the NFL donated $412,500 to wounded-warrior projects, and was lavishly praised by partner networks for doing so. The amount is about one-twentieth of one percent of the league's annual public subsidy.

In addition to subsidies to build and operate stadia, and to taxpayers' money channeled through the defense budget, the NFL enjoys many special forms of government protection: prominently, a congressional waiver that exempts the league from antitrust laws. Basically the waiver allows the NFL to enforce monopoly pricing in television contracts. Without this special deal, the cost of pro football broadcast rights would fall

---

*The NBA and MLB also may have military color guards at their events, seemingly a way to divert attention from the public subsidies they, too, receive, though at a lower level than the NFL.

and cable carrier fees charged to consumers would go down. The antitrust waiver shafts average people in order to create higher profits for NFL owners.

As this book went to press the Bucs, Chargers, Dolphins, Raiders, Rams, Saints and the Washington franchise,[*] were pressuring local governments either for new publicly financed stadia or for substantial taxpayer investments to upgrade existing facilities. Several members of this group were threatening to move to Los Angeles, the largest American city without an NFL franchise, if they did not receive a megabucks Christmas present from taxpayers. When some NFL team does relocate to the City of Angels, the remainder of the NFL ownership class will be sad, since they will no longer be able to twist arms for subsidies by threatening to move there.[†]

At this writing, competing projects in the near-Los Angeles cities of Carson and Inglewood were angling to land relocating NFL teams. One would be funded by $1.4 billion in public borrowing, with the NFL tossing in a mere $200 million. The

---

[*] Not only is the name Redskins objectionable, so is the Washington part, since this team practices in Virginia, performs in Maryland, and lacks the decency to even maintain an office in the District of Columbia. As for Redskins, when the name was chosen in 1933, perhaps, "redskin" was acceptable in polite speech. But language evolves and has evolved away from this term. In 1933, some would have contended that calling African Americans "darkies" was not a slur. There's no chance the NFL today would allow a franchise named the Washington Darkies. There's no chance fans would sing "Hail to the Darkies." So why is Washington Redskins okay?

[†] The videogame Madden NFL 15 has a section in which players can compete at being owners. One option to increase subsidies for your franchise is by moving the Colts or Bengals or whichever team you are playing as to Los Angeles.

other would use bookkeeping hocus-pocus to appear to be privately funded: taxpayers would be on the hook to repay capital costs to the stadium developer down the road.

Documents supporting the Inglewood plan claim that a $1.9 billion NFL stadium, mostly funded by taxpayers, would cause $3.8 billion in local economic expansion. This "magic multiplier" fails the giggle test. Many studies, by Long and by others, have shown that for any dollar of civic investment, building roads, bridges, mass transit and other infrastructure has far more multiplier effect than building NFL fields.

Baseball fields can pass a multiplier test, because they cost so much less than NFL stadia and are used so much more often. Professional football fields are a capital-investment double whammy—the dearest kind of sports facility to build, then used the least. Glendale, Arizona, where the most recent Super Bowl was played, funded most of the stadium in which the Arizona Cardinals perform, after receiving magic-multiplier promises. Today the city has trouble hiring police officers and EMTs because 40 percent of its budget goes to retiring stadium debt. The promised magical economic boom did not occur.

In a 2015 study, Ted Gayer and Alex Gold of the Brookings Institution concluded, "Despite the fact that new stadiums are thought to boost local economic growth and job creation, these benefits are often overstated. Academic studies typically find no discernible positive relationship between sports facility construction and economic development. Most evidence suggests sports subsidies cannot be justified on the grounds of local economic development, income growth or job creation."

In most instances of public subsidies for NFL stadia, state

and local politicians are the bad guys. Mayors, governors, and county commissioners know that if they oppose giveaways to the NFL, they will be accused of being "against football"— while if they spend the public's money lavishly, the painful invoices will not fall due until after they have left office.

When work began in 2000 on the facility now called NRG Stadium, the field where the Houston Texans perform, Houston mayor Lee Brown was an enthusiastic backer. A local stadium authority put $400 million of taxpayers' money into the deal, across from $250 million ponied up by billionaire Bob McNair,* who would keep nearly all revenue from NFL games in the facility. Standing for reelection in 2001, Brown frequently appeared in public with his arm around McNair, and made numerous visits to the stadium construction site, news crews in tow. Associating himself with the pizzazz of the NFL helped Brown win the race. By 2012, Houston civic finances were crippled by long-term deficits. But having served the legal-maximum three terms, Brown had airily departed, leaving debt for someone else to repair.

The whole assumption that taxpayers should support stadia traces to earlier generations when the economics of sports were very different than today.

California's Rose Bowl and Los Angeles Memorial Coliseum were built in the 1920s, at a time that Progressive Era politics contended civic improvement would help bring the country together. Because there was no way to watch games on television, stadia of the period were huge compared to the contemporaneous

---

* Net worth: $2.4 billion, according to *Forbes* magazine.

population—when USC and UCLA faced off at the Los Angeles Memorial Coliseum in 1939 before 103,303 spectators, this was like playing before 1.1 million Californians today.

Football stadia of this era were conceptualized as akin to libraries and parks: college teams would be performing for the public's benefit, tickets would be cheap so anyone could attend. Bearing in mind that all money figures in this book are stated in today's dollars, 50-yard line seats at the 1939 USC-UCLA contest cost $38. Through the 1930s, football facilities such as Buffalo's War Memorial Stadium were built in large part to create construction jobs to counter the Depression, and were priced as public goods. When I attended Bills games at War Memorial as a boy, the bleachers were $7 per head, the best seats in the house $45.

After the 1930s came World War II, with all economic activity diverted to military materiel. During the 1950s, the primary concern of nearly all levels of government was building housing and highway infrastructure for returning veterans; the secondary concern, expansion of state university systems.

By the 1960s, interest was growing in a new wave of stadia for professional football. There still was relatively little television money in NFL coffers: most owners could not have afforded to pay for a field on their own, and lacked the clout to arrange financing. Government help was required. This situation—NFL can't afford to build a new stadium on its own—persisted through the 1970s or into the 1980s, depending on the franchise in question.

By the current generation, every NFL owner could pay for his or her new stadium, and now capital markets can arrange financing unassisted. Yet the many-decades-old assumption that taxpayers should support football stadium construction continues. Owners take advantage of the belief, on the part of taxpayers, that public money ought to be employed to build or upgrade NFL stadia. In the twenty-first century, this belief is archaic nonsense. But so long as politicians act as if the assumption were still valid, why should NFL owners dissent? Local pols and civic leaders are more to blame for the situation than NFL owners.

Taxpayer subsidies for NFL fields are offensive both because the league can now afford to pay its own way, and because ordinary people are paying to build facilities so nice that they're priced out of ever using them.

In September 2014, when Fox staged its initial 49ers telecast from the gleaming new Levi's Stadium, play-by-play man Joe Buck marveled, "They spared no expense on this stadium." *They* being California taxpayers who were watching on TV because *they* couldn't afford to come in, with 2014 season tickets selling for $2,850 to $14,000 per seat.

In 2014, the average NFL ticket cost $85, twice the inflation-adjusted cost of a generation ago. Parking at $25, beer at $12, and soft drinks at $9 are common, with nearly all concession revenue kept by NFL owners. Team Marketing Report, a Chicago consultancy, calculated that in 2014 a family of four spent $635 to attend a Dallas Cowboys home game sitting in regular seats, not in a suite or on a premium concourse; $625 for the same family to attend a Patriots home game; $600 for a Washington home game. That typical people are taxed to fund NFL facilities, yet only the expense-account set can afford to enter, ought to be a source of populist uproar.

The kicker is that after reaching into the pockets of American taxpayers for subsidies, the National Football League offers better deals to viewers in Canada and Mexico than in the United States.

Here's what happens. Local affiliates almost always show games involving nearby teams, even if those games are dogs and better pairings are available. For example, one Sunday late in the 2014 season, most of the country saw Detroit at New England, a matchup of playoff-bound top teams. But Florida, Illinois and parts of Kentucky saw the Bears, already eliminated from the postseason, versus the woeful Bucs, who would finish the season 2-14. Viewers were given no choice in the matter.

In theory, pro football enthusiasts can opt out of the local affiliates and choose the game they wish to watch by purchasing NFL Sunday Ticket, a pay-per-view channel. Sunday Ticket is expensive, $199 to $359 per year to watch games in stadiums you've already been taxed to support. Sunday Ticket is offered only on DirecTV, a satellite carrier. DirecTV requires a dish antenna with an unobstructed view toward the sky above Texas, where the company's satellite hangs. For roughly half the households in the United States there is no unobstructed view of the sky in that direction, rendering subscribing to DirecTV impossible. People who live around trees, or in city centers with tall buildings, cannot opt for Sunday Ticket.

If Sunday Ticket were available via cable, this problem would be solved. But since the inception of the service, in 1994, the NFL has always sold an exclusive right to DirecTV, which pays a pretty penny—$1.5 billion in 2015—because DirecTV would go out of business without Sunday Ticket as the star attraction for its marketing.

Step one: take taxpayer subsidies to build and operate NFL stadia. Step two: price average people out of attending games. Step three: create a cartel to prevent millions of Americans from choosing which games they want to watch on TV. Step four: sit back as Congress does nothing.

In Canada and Mexico, communication laws prohibit the kind of cartel arrangement the NFL has with DirecTV regarding Sunday Ticket. So viewers in Canada and Mexico, who have paid nothing to support the NFL, enjoy freedom to watch whatever NFL game they choose by ordering Sunday Ticket over cable. In the United States, where voters are taxed to subsidize NFL profits, most football fans do not have free choice.

To reduce consumer-advocate pressure regarding Sunday Ticket, in 2014 the NFL announced the service would become available via broadband, no satellite dish and sky sightlines required. Many news organizations swallowed this hook, line, and sinker, running articles saying that at last anyone could get Sunday Ticket. In the fine print of the NFL offer: broadband access available only to those in dorms at "10 select universities, or who live in select areas in one of the following metro cities: New York City, Philadelphia, or San Francisco." Going into the 2015 season, the NFL once again said broadband access to Sunday Ticket would expand. On the day I wrote this paragraph, I tried to sign up. I got this message from the Sunday Ticket Web site: SORRY, YOUR ADDRESS IS NOT ELIGIBLE. I've had a DirecTV supervisor at my house, and he verified that it is impossible to sight the satellite from my neighborhood.

THE GAME'S NOT OVER

AT&T'S 2015 purchase of DirecTV was partly to acquire its cartel lock on NFL viewing. When AT&T made the bid for DirecTV, a merger that required the Justice Department's blessing, consumer groups hoped federal regulators would end the Sunday Ticket monopoly arrangement as part of the terms for approval. But Congress isn't the only watchdog that's sound asleep. Barack Obama's Justice Department rolled over and played dead—busily indicting FIFA soccer officials in Switzerland, but granting the NFL free reign to abuse taxpayers at home.

There's no law of nature that says the NFL, or any professional sport, must be publicly subsidized: no law of nature that says every pro sports franchise owner must be a billionaire.

If the NFL paid its own way, income to owners, and salaries for players and coaches, would decline. Owners would still be rich, just not super-rich at public expense. Players and coaches would still be highly compensated, just not instant millionaires. Taxpayers would no longer be fleeced. Less-dazzling amounts of money for a privileged few, combined with a better deal for taxpayers and average fans, would be good for the long-term prospects of the National Football League. (The same reasoning applies to the NBA and MLB.)

Having the NFL pay its own way would lead to a healthier relationship between Americans and their favorite sport. Fans might find they are prouder of their favorite NFL teams than they are today.

# Captain Kirk Will Be an NFL Fan

Two centuries from now, when the United Federation of Planets prepares to launch the starship *Enterprise* on a five-year mission to explore strange new worlds, there will be all manner of technical challenges: not least, surely, broadcasting National Football League games to a vessel moving faster than the speed of light.

Though the NFL is riven with problems, the league is here to stay. America's love affair with the National Football League should continue far into the future.

Turns of events may cut into the NFL's dominance. The rising median age of the United States, for example, could result in a comeback for quiet, serene baseball as the national pastime. Some entirely new athletic challenge may capture the public's attention. With all major team sports dating to the nineteenth century or earlier—soccer traces back to the ancient Greeks—we're due for an invention.

Concussion issues may discourage high schools from sponsoring football, or render liability coverage unaffordable to

THE GAME'S NOT OVER

public school districts. There could be more NFL scandals in
the works, including abuse of narcotic painkillers by current and
former NFL players.* The future may hold some bolt-out-of-
the-blue that makes the NFL look really bad. A saturation
point simply may be reached, at which the profusion of college
and pro games on TV makes it hard even for football enthusiasts to care about the next kickoff.

But the NFL's popularity is sufficiently deep in the national
psyche—a part of America's understanding of our place in the
world—that professional football should be long-lived. And the
NFL has so much money, the league can buy its way out of any
legal entanglements.

People will continue to complain about the NFL: too loud,
too ferocious, too expensive, too subsidized, too superficial, too
self-aggrandizing, too hypocritical, too protected by political
favors, just too much. All true. But people will keep watching.
The acid test of any product is quality. And NFL product quality—the games themselves—is very high.

Prizefighting once had immense popularity in the United
States. In 1936, the whole country gathered 'round the radio to
listen to the first Joe Lewis-Max Schmeling bout. This sport, if
sport it is, still exists, and still is followed by persons of certain
tastes, if taste they have. But prizefighting fell out of fashion
and no longer commands a mass audience. The fights came to
be seen as barbaric: in prizefighting, harm is not a byproduct of
the event, rather, the purpose. The brutality of prizefighting is
too graphic: blood, swollen eyes, dementia in young men. As the

* Details of this issue are in my 2013 book *The King of Sports*.

country grew better-educated, shunning prizefighting became a sign of intelligence.

What happened to prizefighting won't happen to professional football for several reasons. One is that the physical harm done to NFL players rarely is visible in the manner of harm to boxers. Our society reacts to images more than to words, and words about NFL players ("suffered a compound fracture of the fibula") do not convey disgust in the way photographs of boxers' smashed faces do.

Football enfolds a cerebral component—a living chessboard with twenty-two pieces—while prizefighting is just about strength and stamina. Nearly every high school has a football team, which means tens of millions of Americans attend a high school football contest each year and root for a friend, relative or representative of an alma mater. Some schools sponsor boxing clubs. But there's nothing like the mass-scale high school involvement with football.

Basketball might surpass football, being less dangerous, a lot less expensive to stage and possessed of international appeal. But bear in mind that a generation ago, the NBA was widely expected to leapfrog the NFL with American audiences, and this did not happen. Soccer is the most-watched sport worldwide, but not even David Beckham could get Americans to attend soccer games. Once every fourth year during a World Cup seems about all the soccer U.S. audiences crave, and this may remain so despite an influx of immigrants from soccer-loving nations. The majority of immigrants want to become real live nephews of their Uncle Sam, which entails following gridiron football.

That the NFL specifically, and football generally, are around for the long haul is different from saying either is fine as is. Progress has been made in reducing deliberate helmet-to-helmet hits. Many more reforms are needed:

**Youth football.** The NFL should stop encouraging children below middle-school age to join tackle football leagues. Either state legislatures, or Congress, should ban full-pads full-contact football for those younger than thirteen years.

No matter how well-run a youth league may be, it's insane for the United States to condone an activity that causes large numbers of little kids to injure their brains. No ten-year-old, intoxicated by a fantasy of NFL stardom, can appreciate the risks involved. Society does not allow the very young to smoke, drink, drive or engage in other behavior that adults may choose. Society should not allow the very young to put on helmets and bash each other's heads.

**High school football.** The National Federation of State High School Associations, which writes the rulebook for most prep play, was several years ahead of the NFL in imposing rules to reduce vicious hits. But enforcement needs to be stricter. High school football officials, underpaid and often harassed by spectators, as a group need to take their jobs more seriously.

Recent news on the high school front is positive. The state athletic sanctioning boards in California and Texas have mandated big reductions in the hours of live contact practice that high school teams may conduct. Fewer hours of live contact means fewer concussions and fewer injuries of all types. Because

California and Texas are centers of high school football culture, their actions have led many states to reduce live-contact hours.

But there's a long way to go. In the last decade, most states have begun to allow nearly unlimited "optional" (meaning mandatory) high school football film meetings, conditioning sessions, 7 on 7 camps and the like.* A generation ago, high school football ended around Thanksgiving and resumed in the sweltering heat of August: coaches were forbidden to stage team sessions in the winter and spring. Now, in most states, high school football is year-round. Concurrent with this, promoters have begun to present an interminable parade of "showcases" and "combines" that ostensibly help boys gain the notice of recruiters but actually are all about the fees paid to the promoters for entry. Way too much time spent on high school football distracts boys from the GPAs and balanced extracurriculars needed to gain regular admission to college when, as is almost always the case, recruiters do not come calling.

The NFL could play a leadership role here both by sending its officials and coaches to meet with state sanctioning boards and urging them to restrict the high school football off-season, and by running a public awareness campaign on this score. But the NFL adopts a three-monkeys approach to the issues of prep football—the league sees nothing, hears nothing, speaks nothing. Pro owners view high school football as a training organization run at someone else's expense, and as a way to generate more fans. Responsibility needs to be taken.

---

* Any high school boy who hopes to start knows he'd best be present at every "optional" off-season team session.

**College.** NCAA football issues such as whether players should be paid are beyond the scope of this book. But everyone agrees that college football players ought to be receiving an education. They're not. The two most recent Division 1 college champions are Ohio State, with a 64 percent graduation rate for football players, and Florida State, with a 53 percent football graduation rate.[*]

Academics has long been treated as a big joke by the NCAA. But the joke isn't funny, and every year seems to be in worse taste.

After the most recent NFL season, San Francisco 49ers coach Jim Harbaugh moved to the University of Michigan head coaching job. His contract confers a $150,000 bonus if players achieve "academic excellence." Excellence is measured by the NCAA's Academic Progress Rate, a metric not used in any other aspect of higher education, invented by the NCAA to shift the conversation away from diplomas. Harbaugh receives his bonus for "excellence" if the team APR reaches 960. Since college football programs average 951 on this metric, at the University of Michigan "academic excellence" has been defined down to just barely above average. Harbaugh's contract offers no incentive for him to alter Michigan's dismal 59 percent graduation rate for football, but does pay him about $7 million per year, with nearly $1 million in bonuses for victories, plus use of a private jet.

The NFL cannot control college-conference or NCAA de-

---

[*] These poor numbers are not caused by juniors leaving early for the NFL. These two programs combined had a total of four early-entrant departures in their title years, a minor factor in graduation rates.

cision-making, but could set a good example regarding education. Instead, the NFL stages combines and issues draft forecasts to college players, diverting their focus from the classroom to sports. The draft forecasts, issued in December of collegians' junior year, consistently overstate the likelihood of being selected—luring players to surrender their scholarships and then discover themselves unemployed.* The NFL benefits from the maximum number of prospects entering the draft pool. That encouraging college players to surrender scholarships in return for not making a professional roster screws the collegian is something the NFL does not care about in the slightest.

NFL press guides and rosters list players by colleges regardless of whether they graduated. This creates an illusion that football players get educations, earn diplomas, then go on to exciting professional careers. Only about 50 percent of NFL players are college graduates; all are presented to the public by the league, and by their teams, as members of the Joe College set. A simple truth-in-advertising rule, requiring the NFL to list players by their high schools if they failed to graduate from college, would help the public grasp the situation.

**The NFL.** In the last five years, the league has changed from denying health issues to taking steps in the right direction: a

---

* For example, in 2010, the NFL told junior Donovan Warren he'd be a first-round choice if he jumped, and told junior Jevan Snead he'd be no lower than a third. Both gave up their scholarships and were not drafted. I wrote on ESPN, "Something with the grandiose name NFL Draft Advisory Committee, composed of high league officials, sounds to impressionable college kids like a fast lane to fame and fortune. But the advisory board is only guessing, and draft guesswork is often wrong."

crackdown on deliberate helmet-to-helmet hits, strict unsports-manlike conduct penalties, independent neurologists and medical spotters with authority to pull players from games. These reforms reduce risk to professionals. More importantly, they set a good example for high school and college football, which imitate the NFL.

Here is what needs to come next, for the NFL first and then for all levels of the sport: eliminate kickoffs, and eliminate the three-point and four-point stances.

Kickoffs are the most concussion-prone down, because players running at full speed from opposite directions crash into each other.[*] Kickoffs are a bad down for knee injuries, too. In 2011, the NFL moved the kickoff spot from the kicking team's 30 to 35, in order to increase touchbacks and, by reducing kickoff returns, reduce concussions.

Touchbacks—now there's an exciting play! If the goal is to increase touchbacks, let's have done and eliminate the kickoff. After a score, the other team takes possession on its 25-yard line. In order to retain the last-minute onside kick and kickoff excitement in the final moments generally, kickoffs could be confined to the final two minutes of each half.

If the NFL eliminated kickoffs, or confined them to the final two minutes, college and high school likely would follow. Concussions would be reduced—both in games and in practice, since teams would cut back on time practicing kickoff returns.

A hidden problem with the kickoff return is that special teams' players usually are reserves who hurl themselves around

---

[*] Punt returns have a different dynamic—most players are running in the same direction, not in opposite directions.

recklessly, trying to impress the coaches. At the prep level, the backups, who aren't going to get a college admission boost from football, are most likely to hurt themselves while doing something rash on a kickoff runback. Eliminating or greatly reducing the opportunity for recklessness would be a big step forward for America's 1.1 million high school players. The NFL should lead the way.

Once, basketball held a jump ball after each field goal. When in 1938 the jump ball after each field goal was eliminated, purists howled. When in 1982 jump balls after simultaneous control were eliminated too, replaced by the possession arrow, purists nodded with approval. By that juncture the jump ball was viewed as obsolescent. The same is in store for football's kickoff.

As for the "down" stance of one or both hands on the ground, look at any picture of an NFL play about to start. Five offensive linemen usually (not always) have a hand on the ground; two to five defenders have one or two hands on the ground. At the snap, the guys with their hands on the ground smash heads. The physics of the down stance makes this inevitable, since the stance causes a head-against-head alignment.

There were 32,779 offensive snaps in the 2014 NFL regular season. That's a lot of head-bangs. Multiply this times tens of thousands of annual college and high school football games.

If the down stance were banned, every player would begin the play with head up, rather than the linemen beginning the play with their heads pointed at the opponent's heads. Brain trauma would decline—especially long-term cumulative trauma, since research increasingly shows it's lots of routine impacts, not one spectacular knockout hit, that does the most neurological harm.

As with kickoffs, if the NFL banned the down stance, the NCAA and prep leagues would follow. Banning the three-point stance would be a leader-institution move for the NFL.

Purists will say, "Never!" Yet look closely before a snap. Increasingly in the NFL, many offensive linemen set in a two-point stance because it's better for pass protection. Sometimes only one or two defensive linemen have their hands on the ground because the standup stance is better for the zone-rush schemes that are a recent rage among defensive coordinators. This suggests the three-point stance is going out of style anyway. If the down stance were banned, the game would be every bit as exciting, while becoming somewhat less dangerous. Within a generation, down-stance football would be forgotten—consigned to the sports museum, along with the jump ball.

Possible compromise: allow hands on the ground at the snap only on fourth downs.

**Three more NFL Reforms.** The league should switch to a seeded postseason tournament format. In 2014, the Carolina Panthers finished with a losing record and hosted a playoff game, while the 10-6 Eagles and four 9-7 teams did not advance to the postseason. In 2008, 8-8 San Diego hosted a playoff contest while 12-4 Indianapolis opened on the road and 11-5 New England did not advance to the postseason. There are many like examples in NFL annals.

Divisions could be still be employed to organize schedules and preserve rivalries. But after the regular season, teams should be seeded by records. Losers should not advance while winners stay home—that's un-American!

The most entertaining event in contemporary sports, and a ratings beast, is the NCAA men's March Madness bracket, which is a seeded tournament. This format provides excitement while maximizing the chance of the best two teams meeting in the finale contest, as happened in 2015 when the Duke and Wisconsin teams, the two best in men's basketball, met for the title game.

If a seeded NFL tournament resulted in two NFC or two AFC clubs squaring off in the Super Bowl, so be it. The NFC-AFC Super Bowl rivalry is long past. Most football enthusiasts don't even know where that rivalry stands now, or care.

Next reform: the NFL should disclose, by team, the total amount of prescription painkillers used. Not by individual player—medical privacy would be preserved. Simply disclose the team's annual cumulative totals for opioid painkillers, in-jected Toradol (little known to the public, disturbingly common in NFL locker rooms) and local anesthesia administered to joints. All NFL teams have staff doctors with prescribing priv-ileges; many have what amount to on-site pharmacies where doctors or trainers distribute controlled substances.[*] Just dis-close the total amount used each season. It is likely the public, and Congress, will be shocked.

A last recommended NFL reform: Congress should amend copyright law such that professional sports leagues cannot copyright images made in publicly funded facilities. The devil

---

[*] The New Orleans Saints paid a federal fine after large amounts of Vico-din disappeared from the team's on-site pharmacy. In 2014, Drug Enforce-ment Administration officers questioned officials of the Buccaneers, 49ers and Seahawks about team use of narcotic painkillers.

would be in the details of such a legal shift. But the effect on the NFL would be immediate and profound. The league would scramble to pay back every dime of subsidies to existing stadia, and never ask for construction or operations handouts again. This would, in one fell swoop—whatever that means*—resolve the number-one public policy objection to the National Football League, placing the NFL into the healthy relationship with taxpayers that was dreamed about in the previous chapter.

This book began by proposing that the National Football League has assumed such an outsized role in United States life both because the games are so good and because the NFL holds up a mirror to the internal conflicts of American society.

The first factor, the quality of the games, extends beyond the outstanding skills of players. As a living chessboard, professional football engages the mind. Many sports offer interesting action but few regularly cause the audience to say, "I wonder what strategy will be used next?" Strategy choices in the NFL make for talk radio, water-cooler and tavern debate. No other team game draws the spectator into tactics in the way professional football does.

Some professional sports offer impressive athletic performance (basketball). Some offer tactics and number-crunching (baseball). Some offer speed (ice hockey), some stamina (soccer). Some create a pleasing make-believe world (golf). Only football has all these qualities. The NFL's combination of

---

* Maybe it would happen in one swell foop.

strength, speed, power and thinking results in the perfect sport for a strong nation of rising education levels.

The NFL shows the reflection of a broad range of issues in society. Some, such as gay marriage or handling of domestic violence, may fade as a social consensus is reached. But the question of America's proper role in the world will be with us for generations, and is reflected in the king of sports.

The United States is a musclebound superpower that's never really sure how to behave. Professional football is a musclebound superpower sport that can't make up its mind what's right, either. The United States and professional football were made for each other. And we'll take this most American of games with us when we head to the stars.

# Memorable Moments in Professional Football

**1965**—Buffalo Bills quarterback Jack Kemp is Player of the Year as the Bills defeat the San Diego Chargers for the old American Football League title. Kemp would go on to become a member of Congress, then Secretary of Housing and Urban Development during the presidency of the elder George Bush, then 1996 Republican Party candidate for vice-president. This places Kemp on the short list of athletes whose major life achievements began after taping the ankles for the final time.

**1966**—The National Football League and rival American Football League agree to merge.

**1967**—The Green Bay Packers defeat the Kansas City Chiefs in the inaugural AFL-NFL Championship. Later the event's nickname, Super Bowl, would be the formal name. The Super Bowl—maybe you've heard of it?

**1968**—The nation comes to a halt when NBC switches off the tense final minute of the Jets-Raiders contest now known as the Heidi Game. Yodelers, however, are happy.

**1969**—NFL Offensive Rookie of the Year is Dallas's Calvin Hill—a true son of Yale University and a graduate of its halls before his first NFL practice. As recently as the 1970s, the annual Harvard-Yale game packed the seventy-one-thousand-seat Yale Bowl; today Ivy League football remains a pleasure, plus it's easy to park. Footnote: Hill played in the same Bulldogs backfield as Brian Dowling, who was the inspiration for B.D., the hapless quarterback in the *Doonesbury* comic strip.

**1970**—The Kansas City Chiefs defeat the Minnesota Vikings in the Super Bowl with a touchdown on 65 Toss Power Trap, among cognoscenti the best-known play name in football.

**1971**—Defensive tackle Alan Page of the Vikings is the first defender (and so far, only one of two, with Lawrence Taylor, in 1986, the other) to win the NFL MVP award. Page played at 245 pounds—today, defensive tackles at that weight are unheard-of even in college football. Later Page would graduate from law school and become a justice on the Minnesota state Supreme Court, joining Kemp as an NFL star whose important life achievements occurred after sports.

MVP footnote: Peyton Manning has received this award five times, but won the Super Bowl only once. Terry Bradshaw and Joe Montana have eight Super Bowl victories between them, but two fewer MVP trophies than Manning.

**1972**—The Miami Dolphins finish 17-0, the NFL's sole perfect season. They do this with no one on the roster above 300 pounds. The most recent Super Bowl victor, the New England Patriots of 2015, had eleven players above 300 pounds.

**1973**—Broadway choreographer Texie Waterman is hired by the Dallas Cowboys to bring a showgirl mentality to cheerleading. At the time, cheerleaders were modest, even frumpy. Soon the bombshell cheer-babe would become the NFL norm.

**1974**—The Raiders, hosting Miami in the playoffs, trailed by 5 points with a few seconds remaining. No one thought Oakland could triumph: the Dolphins had been to three consecutive Super Bowls, winning two. Oakland quarterback Ken "The Snake" Stabler, renowned for improvising—he was allergic to the playbook—scrambled around, then heave-hoed a crazy pass caught by Clarence Davis in the end zone, preventing Miami from a fourth straight Super Bowl appearance. In the contest the defending champion Dolphins rushed forty-one times and dropped back to pass sixteen times—then a standard ratio, today the reverse of standard tactics.

**1975**—The eight-team postseason field includes the St. Louis Cardinals, Baltimore Colts and Los Angeles Rams, none of which exist in the 2015 season.

**1976**—The Tampa Bay Buccaneers fail to score five times on the way to finishing 0-14, the first winless team of the fourteen-game-season format. (In 2008, the Detroit Lions would grab the sixteen-game-season brass ring at 0-16.) Perhaps the worst woofer in NFL annals occurs when the Bucs, soon to be 0-14, meet the Seahawks, who would finish 2-12.

**1977**—The Bears' Walter Payton rushes for 275 yards, then the most ever in a game. The contest was played at Soldier Field before a delirious crowd that chanted "SWEET-ness! SWEET-ness!"—Sweetness was Payton's nickname—as he neared the record. Thirty years later, Adrian Peterson would run for 296 yards in an NFL game, at this writing the record.

**1978**—The NFL makes the first of three sets of rule changes that encourage more forward passes. Before the 1978 rulebook rewrite, NFL games were 45 percent passing. By 1999, games would be 57 percent passing.

**1979**—Veteran Jackie Smith, thirty-eight years old, comes out of retirement to be the backup tight end for the Dallas Cowboys; does not catch a pass all season; makes his only Super Bowl appearance when Dallas faces Pittsburgh; is open in the end zone for the touchdown that would win the Super Bowl; and drops a perfectly thrown pass.

**1980**—Cleveland hosts Oakland in the playoffs with a kickoff temperature of 4 degrees Fahrenheit, the coldest game since the 1967 Ice Bowl in Green Bay. Trailing by 2 points, the Browns reach the Raiders' 13-yard line with 49 ticks showing. A field goal wins the game, but extreme cold makes field goals harder as air condenses. Run! Run! Pass intercepted, and so begins the Browns' unhappy decade of last-second playoff frustration.

1981—Jim Plunkett leads Oakland to a Super Bowl ring, the first of two he would earn with the Raiders. Plunkett, whose Mexican grandparents make him the lone Latino Super Bowl MVP, began his career as the first-overall choice in the NFL draft; then was traded to the San Francisco 49ers for a king's ransom (three number-one draft choices plus change), then was waived by the 49ers. After winning the Super Bowl for Oakland, Plunkett was benched, returning for his second Lombardi Trophy only when Oakland's starter was injured. Plunkett is the sole quarterback to direct two Super Bowl wins who is not in the Hall of Fame: the knocks on him are that he was fabulous in the playoffs but had a career losing record during the regular season, and that he threw more interceptions than touchdown passes. Joe Namath is in the Hall of Fame despite a career losing record in the regular season and more interceptions than touchdowns thrown, and one less Super Bowl ring than Plunkett.

1982—The Catch, Montana-to-Clark with seconds remaining as the 49ers defeat the favored Cowboys in the NFC championship. This victory makes the name of the pass-first West Coast Offense that soon would dominate football. The play call was Red Right Tight Sprint Right. Today, the NFL's bells-and-chimes theme that precedes each broadcast is titled *Sprint Right.*

**1983**—The Class of '83, best quarterback year ever for the NFL draft. Stars John Elway, Jim Kelly and Dan Marino are chosen, along with several other quarterbacks who became quality NFL performers.

**1984**—Marino starts in the Super Bowl as a rookie, but the Dolphins are outgunned by Joe Montana's 49ers, who finish the season 18-1.

**1985**—The Los Angeles Rams and Los Angeles Raiders make the playoffs but don't reach the last contest, precluding a Subway Super Bowl—or a Freeway Super Bowl, considering Los Angeles. The Jets and Giants have never met in the Super Bowl either. Since neither actually plays in New York City, if they did meet in the NFL's final contest, it would be the Jersey Turnpike Bowl.

**1986**—Struggling a bit halfway through the regular season, the Chicago Bears release the Super Bowl Shuffle, a music video in which Bears' stars gyrated while singing, if that term may be applied loosely. Purists were outraged: the public loved it. Impressed, the football gods smile on the team. The Bears win the Super Bowl on the strength of what many consider the best-ever defense, holding the Patriots to a meager 2.3 yards per offensive snap, while posting six takeaways. Chicago boasted four future Hall of Fame players—Dan Hampton, Richard Dent, Walter Payton and Mike Singletary—plus a future Hall of Fame coach in Mike Ditka. The Bears finish 18-1, matching the 49ers for most-ever wins.

**1987**—A weekly Sunday night game begins on national prime time. Expected to be a flop, by 2010 *Sunday Night Football* would become the nation's highest-rated TV show. In the AFC title game, the Denver Broncos drive 98 yards, ultimately scoring in the closing seconds of regulation versus the Cleveland Browns, and go on to win in overtime. The Drive joins The Catch in football lore, while for Browns' fans, lamentations continue. In Cleveland, there is rending of garments and gnashing of teeth.

**1988**—Not long after being let go by the Arizona Outlaws of the defunct USFL, Doug Williams becomes the first African American quarterback to win the Super Bowl MVP award, playing for the Washington franchise.

**1989**—The Vikings block a Rams punt out of the end zone in overtime, the first overtime contest in NFL annals decided by a safety. (This has happened twice more since.[*]) The final was Vikings 23, Rams 21—Minnesota putting up 23 points without scoring a touchdown.

**1990**—The Run and Shoot offense is the NFL's fad of the season: four wide receivers, no tight end. This craze precedes later fashions for the no-huddle, the five-wide, the shotgun spread, and eventually, the Philadelphia Eagles' warp-speed Blur Offense.

---

[*] Owing to rules differences, an overtime safety is all but impossible in high school and NCAA football.

**1991**—Using a no-huddle offense the entire game, then a revolutionary notion, the Buffalo Bills defeat the Oakland Raiders 51-3 in the AFC title contest. The national broadcast is repeatedly interrupted by news reports of air raid sirens in Saudi Arabia, as the 1991 Gulf War begins. A week later, Buffalo loses the Super Bowl to the Giants on the most famous missed field goal in gridiron annals.* The Bills would appear in four consecutive Super Bowls, the only team to do so, but their no-huddle always ran out of gas at the last, leading to the woe-for-four streak.

**1992**—Out injured for most of two seasons, Joe Montana comes off the bench in the 49ers' final regular season contest and plays well. Steve Young regains the job in the postseason, and San Francisco loses to Dallas in the NFC title game. San Francisco coaches prefer Young; Montana is traded away to prevent home fans from chanting for him.

**1993**—Trailing the Houston Oilers 35-3 in the second half in the playoffs, the Buffalo Bills complete the greatest comeback in NFL annals. Key play: on a fourth-and-long, when standard tactics said to do the "safe" thing and attempt a field goal, Bills coach Marv Levy called four verticals, meaning all receivers streak deep. Touchdown, and Houston never recovered. In Super Bowls, Levy would do the "safe" thing and punt, leading to defeat—see Bonus #2.

---

* This was not an Erie Canal Super Bowl because the Giants were already playing in New Jersey. The "New York" Giants moved to Jersey in 1976, the "New York" Jets to Jersey in 1984. For three decades the Buffalo Bills have been New York state's sole NFL franchise.

**1994**—Heath Shuler, chosen third overall in the NFL draft, becomes a bust as a football player but would later serve North Carolina for three terms in the House of Representatives.

**1995**—The Kansas City Chiefs post a league-best 13-3 regular season record, then wheeze out in the postseason, scoring just 7 points in a playoff-opening home loss.

**1996**—Dom Capers, coach of the Carolina Panthers, is named NFL Coach of the Year. Two years later he would be fired—what have you done for us lately? Capers's resume includes coaching jobs at Kent State, the University of Washington, the University of Hawaii, San Jose State, Cal, the University of Tennessee, Ohio State, the Baltimore Stars of the USFL, the New Orleans Saints, the Pittsburgh Steelers, the Panthers, the Jacksonville Jaguars, the Houston Texans, the Miami Dolphins, the New England Patriots and the Green Bay Packers. Sixteen employers in fourteen states doesn't make him weird, it makes him normal in the peripatetic world of football coaching.

**1997**—Again the Kansas City Chiefs are 13-3 in the regular season, then again wheeze out in the postseason, this time putting up all of 10 points in a home opening-round loss. A team loaded with stars—Marcus Allen, Joe Montana, Andre Rison, Will Shields, Derrick Thomas—would in the 1990s be 102-58 in the regular season but 3-7 in the postseason, a study in frustration.

**1998**—John Elway's Broncos defeat Brett Favre's Packers in a Super Bowl pairing of Hall of Fame quarterbacks. A year later, after Denver defeated Atlanta for a consecutive Lombardi Trophy, Elway immediately retired, going out in style. He saved the best for last!

1999—Linebacker Dat Nguyen of the Dallas Cowboys becomes the first Vietnamese-American to start in the NFL. Five-foot-nine-inch Doug Flutie throws for 360 yards for Buffalo versus Miami in the playoffs, but with seconds remaining, fumbles at the Dolphins' goal line.

2000—Kurt Warner is Super Bowl MVP for the Rams just two years after he'd been a bagger at a grocery store. A vagabond coach named Tony Franklin begins selling an instruction manual showing high schools how to run a quick-snap spread offense. By the end of the decade, this style takes over football from the prep to pro levels.

2001—The Vikings face the Giants in the NFC title game. Giants coaches had drawn up an unusual play in which blocking back Greg Comella split wide, then ran a deep fade route: fullbacks who split wide are almost always decoys. New York scored on its first possession, then Minnesota fumbled the ensuing kickoff.* Home crowd roaring, Giants' coach Jim Fassel screamed "Use it now!" to his quarterback. A long touchdown pass to Comella turned the game into a walkover—an example of perfect playcalling.

A few months later, Michael Vick became the first African

---

* Sportswriting prevents "ensuing" from fading from usage.

American quarterback to be the number-one choice of the NFL draft, ending a century of a WHITES ONLY sign on the quarterback position.

2002—Super Bowl tied with 1:30 remaining, underdog New England takes possession on its 17-yard line, Patriots and Rams both out of timeouts. Announcer John Madden, Hall of Fame coach and video-game impresario, tells the national television audience New England should just kneel on the ball and be content to go to overtime, since trying to score fast from this position is risky. But victories don't come in the mail, go win the game! Eight snaps, two of them spikes to stop the clock, plus two crazy all-out Rams blitzes, get the Patriots to the St. Louis 30, where a field goal splits the uprights as time expires.

2003—To begin the season, the Tampa Bay Buccaneers make a high-stakes trade, sending two number-one draft choices, other picks and $8 million to the Oakland Raiders not for any player, but for their coach, Jon Gruden. To end the season, the Raiders and Buccaneers meet in the Super Bowl, with Tampa Bay winning. Afterward, Raiders' players bitterly complain that the team's new coaches did not bother to change the calls installed by Gruden—meaning Tampa defenders knew what was coming.

   The Super Bowl glow doesn't last long. Just four games after winning the Lombardi Trophy, the Buccaneers, leading 35-14 with 5:09 remaining in the fourth quarter at home on *Monday Night Football,* manage to lose to the Indianapolis Colts, who stage a speed-of-light comeback.

**2004**—The New England Patriots defeat the Indianapolis Colts in a playoff contest marred by so much uncalled defensive holding on the part of New England that Aaron Schatz, founder of the independent Web site Football Outsiders, and a diehard Patriots' fan, calls the game "a public mugging by New England." A few months later, NFL rules are changed to clarify that New England's tactics should have resulted in penalties. This is the third of the three sets of rule changes, begun in 1978, to improve the odds of completed passes.

**2005**—Trailing Washington by 1 point with seconds remaining, facing a PAT try, rather than do the "safe" thing and kick, Tampa Bay coach Gruden went for two. The Buccaneers won.

At the end of the season, Jerry Rice retires as arguably football's greatest player. Surely so by stats, because of the margin of his records. Baseball's all-time home run hitter, Barry Bonds, has 1 percent more homers than Hank Aaron at second-best. Basketball's all-time rebounder, Wilt Chamberlain, had 10 percent more rebounds than Bill Russell at second-best. Hockey's all-time leading goal scorer, Wayne Gretzky, had 12 percent more goals than Gordy Howe at second-best. The NFL's all-time rusher, Emmitt Smith, had 10 percent more yards than Walter Peyton at second-best.

Rice? His 1,549 career receptions are 17 percent more than Tony Gonzalez at second-best. His 197 receiving touchdowns are 26 percent more than Randy Moss at second-best. His 22,895 receiving yards are 44 percent more than Terrell Owens at second-best. The distance between Jerry Rice and the second-best at his position is unprecedented in professional sports.

2006—A generation ago, there would have been one nationally televised NFL game and two national college football games per week. Now it's five NFL national TV games and at least thirty national NCAA games. Both numbers will rise.

2007—Brian Westbrook of the Eagles, running for what would be an uncontested touchdown, deliberately stops at the Dallas 1-yard line and kneels, so Philadelphia can kill the clock and end the contest. It's among the top heads-up moves in football annals—from a player who turned down recruiting offers to major college programs so he could attend Villanova and get a real education.

The Patriots are caught using video cameras to steal signals. Bill Belichick claims he thought this was legal—but if it was legal, why did New England elaborately conceal the taping? The Spygate scandal leaves many wondering if professional football has something to hide.

After the season, Troy Brown retires as the last NFL player to play two-way on a regular basis. Brown had 615 catches as a wide receiver plus twenty-two tackles and three interceptions as a defensive back. He also ran back kicks and punts, carried the ball thirty-one times on rushing plays and attempted a pass. (Incomplete.)

2008—In the Super Bowl, the New York Giants defeat the 18-0 Patriots with a touchdown that follows the impossible-to-believe David Tyree helmet catch. New England is the third NFL team to finish 18-1, but without a trophy, it's not the same. Minutes after the contest comes to a close, Reebok airs a

TV ad showing surviving members of the 1972 Dolphins perfect team celebrating.

**2009**—The good news: ESPN ends "Jacked Up," a show that celebrated NFL players bashing each other's heads. The bad news: the NFL continues to sell *highlight videos* of players dropping to the turf unconscious after vicious hits. New Orleans Saints' coaches begin offering players cash for each "cart-off" of injured opponents. After the Saints were caught, head coach Sean Payton would be suspended.

**2010**—Knocked senseless by a concussion but sent back into the game, Philadelphia Eagles linebacker Stewart Bradley staggers around the field clearly having no idea where he is. From this moment on, football concussions are out of the closet.

Brett Favre, the NFL's all-time iron man—297 consecutive starts—takes his final bow. On his very last play, Favre is sacked. To end the season, the New Orleans Saints—Sean Payton not yet suspended—win the Super Bowl largely on the strength of an onside kick to begin the second half. Several Indianapolis Colts players didn't notice the surprise onside because they were watching stage sets for The Who roll off.

**2011**—The Chicago Bears score a touchdown on a punt return trick play that is the prettiest down in pro football history. Chicago's blockers all run in front of Devin Hester as if he's catching the punt, which is actually going to the opposite side of the field. The blockers look upward as if watching the punt approach. This draws the defense toward Hester's side. The guy who actually had the ball ran the length of the field unnoticed. The play was so pretty, who cares if it was nullified by a penalty! Chicago's Corey Graham oversold the fake by holding during a block in front of his teammate, who was only pretending to have the ball.

Ahmad Bradshaw of the Giants wins the Super Bowl when he accidentally scores a touchdown. Bradshaw was supposed to stop at the 1 so New York could run down the clock, then kick a field goal. Patriots' defenders had stepped aside, inviting him to score, and he couldn't resist.

**2012**—The Fail Mary Game. With regular NFL officials locked out, as time expires on *Monday Night Football*, one official signals touchdown (which would win the game for the Seahawks), while the other signals interception (which would win the game for the Packers). Hours after the replacement referee awarded victory to Seattle, the league admits Green Bay should have received the W.

The Baltimore Ravens take the Super Bowl as Joe Flacco throws eleven touchdown passes versus no interceptions in the postseason, including a 70-yard touchdown pass with seconds remaining in regulation to force overtime at Denver.

**2013**—The Miami Dolphins bullying scandal; researchers announce more indications that football causes the degenerative neurological condition CTE; President Barack Obama says, "If I had a son, I wouldn't let him play football." Traditionalists grumble about rule changes to reduce helmet-to-helmet hits, but concussions diminish somewhat while excitement does not.

Peyton Manning's Broncos enter the Super Bowl versus Seattle as the highest scoring team ever, and are held to 8 points in a shellacking. It's part of a pattern of high-scoring teams wheezing out late in the postseason: the Bills in 1991, the Vikings in 1999, the Raiders in 2003, the Patriots in 2008 and the Broncos in 2013.

Linebacker London Fletcher, who should become the first undrafted Division III player to enter the Pro Football Hall of Fame, retires after making 1,796 tackles.

**2014**—The Ray Rice video creates a sense that football is falling apart at the seams. In the playoffs, six-foot-eight-inch, 320-pound New England offensive tackle Nate Solder catches a touchdown pass. Then the NFL season ends with the fascinating, fantastic New England versus Seattle Super Bowl, making the audience long for more.

# Ye Gods, Why Are
# They Punting?

The Minnesota Vikings trailed the New York Giants by 24 points in the 2001 NFC championship game. The Vikings faced fourth-and-inches on their 34. That season, Minnesota had one of the league's best offenses, averaging a top-tier 6.2 yards per snap. So of course the Vikings will go for it; they cannot come back if they are afraid to try to gain one single yard! No way, that absolutely cannot be the punting team trotting in! Boom goes the punt. The result was an epic fail, Minnesota losing the title game 41-0.

Outlier?

The Giants won the 1991 Super Bowl when the Bills' hopes went wide right on the final play. Earlier in the contest, Buffalo punted on fourth-and-1 at midfield, punted on fourth-and-1 at midfield again, then punted on fourth-and-2 *in Giants territory*. That season, the Bills fielded the league's top-ranked offense, which in the 1991 Super Bowl averaged a gold-plated 6.6 yards per snap. Had the Bills simply gone for it on any of the three fourth-and-shorts, the Lombardi Trophy likely would have been theirs to hoist.

Similar examples abound:

In September 2014, Kansas City, loser of four straight to division rival Denver, faced fourth-and-1 at midfield and punted. The day ended with the Chiefs becoming losers of five straight to the Broncos.

The next week, Denver visited Seattle in a rematch of the previous Super Bowl. Trailing by 14 points in the second half, the Broncos, possessed of a high-octane offense, faced fourth-and-1 at midfield. In trotted the punting unit. I don't need to tell you anything else about how that game turned out.

In the 2015 playoffs, the Bengals trailed Indianapolis 26-10 in the fourth quarter. Cincinnati entered the game with the league's longest postseason drought—the last time the Bengals posted a playoff win, the elder George Bush was president. Facing fourth down, Bengals coach Marvin Lewis ordered a punt. Punting while behind in the fourth quarter of a playoff! Needless to say, Indianapolis won. Could such decisions have anything to do with Lewis being 0-6 in the playoffs?

In 2002 the Bills, trailing the Patriots by 10 points, punted on fourth-and-2 *in New England territory*. In 2013 the Bills, trailing the Patriots by 10 points, punted on fourth-and-2 *in New England territory*. Could such decisions have anything to do with Bill Belichick being 26-4 versus Buffalo as New England coach?

These are examples of the Preposterous Punt. Punts on fourth-and-short, when there's a 60 percent chance of a first down, are Preposterous. If there were an exotic blitz that created a 60 percent chance of a turnover, NFL coaches would make that call constantly. Yet though going for it on fourth-

and-short conveys a 60 percent chance of keeping the ball, coaches send in the punt unit—essentially offering the opponent a free turnover.

Whenever a kicking unit trots out on fourth-and-short, the opponent breathes a sigh of relief. This alone tells you the offense should be going for it.

Consider the 2015 NFC championship game, Green Bay at Seattle.

Three times in the first half, Green Bay—with a league-leading 6.2 yards per offensive snap that season—faced fourth-and-1, and all three times sent in the field goal unit. Had the Packers simply gone for it at any of these junctures, the day likely would have ended with them receiving a Super Bowl invitation. But at least field goals generate points. Leading 16-0 in the third quarter, Green Bay faced fourth-and-1 at midfield, and punted. Having survived another offensive series thanks to the Preposterous Punt, the Seahawks outscored their visitors 28-6 for the remainder of the contest. Seattle advanced to the ultimate game.

Now it's two weeks later at the Super Bowl. Seattle leads New England 24-14 early in the fourth quarter and faces fourth-and-2 *in New England territory*. The Seahawks had the league's number-one-rated rushing offense that season, averaging 5.3 yards per carry. Had the Seahawks gone for it, odds are they soon would have been standing in a shower of blue and green confetti. Instead—right after watching the Packers lose by doing the "safe" thing on fourth-and-short—Seattle coaches did the "safe" thing and punted on fourth-and-short. The Patriots outscored the Seahawks 14-0 for the remainder of the contest. The confetti shower was white and red.

Possession of the ball is the most important aspect of football tactics, far more consequential than field position. The Preposterous Punt hands possession to the opponent: the coach might as well instruct his quarterback to throw a deliberate interception.

In the 2013 playoffs the Broncos, boasting the league's number-two offense that season with a 5.8 yards per snap average, were hosting the Ravens. The game went into overtime: Denver faced fourth-and-1 at midfield. Possession of the ball is more important than field position under regular circumstances: in the NFL overtime format, possession of the ball is everything. Boom went the punt, and that's all the information you need to know who won. Of course there are examples of teams punting on fourth-and-1 and being glad they did. In the main, Preposterous Punts correspond with defeat.

In the 2014 regular season, the Bengals, Raiders and Titans were the teams that punted most on fourth-and-short. They finished with a combined 15-33-1 record. That's some "safe" tactic! In the 2014 regular season, NFL teams punted 353 times on fourth-and-2 or fourth-and-1. Since there were 256 regular season contests, that's 1.4 fourth-and-short punts per game—handing the ball back to the opponent rather than taking a 60 percent chance of maintaining possession.

Football analytics provides an open-and-shut case in favor of not punting on fourth-and-short. In 2007, for my Tuesday Morning Quarterback column, the sports analytics firm Accu-Score ran thousands of computer simulations using actual 2006 NFL games with one variable changed: one of the teams in each pairing didn't punt on fourth-and-short. Not launching

Preposterous Punts added an average of 1 point to a team's score, while adding no points to the opponent's scoring.

In the simulation, teams that did not punt on fourth-and-short became 5 percent more likely to win. This translates to nearly one extra W per sixteen-game season. Most NFL owners would pay millions of dollars to win one more game per season. Keep the money in the secret Swiss bank account and tell the coach not to punt on fourth-and-short!

AccuScore then ran ten thousand NFL game simulations to test various down-and-distance decision trees that I proposed. What emerged was this cheat sheet:

Inside your own 20, punt.
From your 21 to 35, go for it on fourth-and-2 or less.
From your 36 to midfield, go for it on fourth-and-3 or less.
Once across midfield, go for it on fourth-and-4 or less.
From the opposition 2 or 1, go for it.
Except: in the fourth quarter, whenever inside your place-
    kicker's reliable range, on fourth down, attempt a field
    goal if three points ties the game or gives you the lead.

Both the statistical-analytical case and the anecdotal case from games such as the 2015 NFC championship and 2015 Super Bowl, offer an overwhelming argument for not launching Preposterous Punts. Yet launch them NFL teams do, in dreary number.

If the case for going for it on fourth-and-short is so strong, why do NFL coaches punt? To shift blame.

Suppose a coach does the manly-man thing and goes for it,

and the try fails: he is slammed by the sportsyak world. Suppose a coach does the "safe" thing, orders a punt, and the team loses: the players are the ones blamed.

In a 2009 game at Indianapolis, the Patriots led the Colts 34-28 just before the two minute warning, facing fourth-and-2 on their own 28. Punting would have handed possession back to the Colts, whose offense had gotten hot in the second half; converting the first down would have allowed New England to drain almost all time off the clock by kneeling. Belichick had the Patriots go for it. The runner was shy by a yard; Indianapolis took over and scored a touchdown to win.

That night and the following week, the sportsyak world methodically scolded Belichick for his decision—which had been the correct call, but just didn't work. In some ways this was a decision only Belichick could have made, since he has the league's most job security. Any other NFL coach might have feared that a fourth-and-short try from his own 28 would get him fired the next morning.* Because punting is expected on fourth-and-short, a coach who does not send out the punt unit is viewed as having committed a huge blunder—even if it's punting that is the actual blunder.

Contrast Belichick being raked over the coals about his Indianapolis call with the 1991 Super Bowl. Sports commentators taunted Scott Norwood, who missed the winning field-goal attempt, and mocked those players of the heavily favored Bills who dropped passes and missed tackles because, overconfident,

---

* In 2014, Kliff Kingsbury, coach of the Texas Tech football program, said, "Give me a 10-year guaranteed contract and I would never send out the punter."

they'd been out clubbing till the wee hours the morning of the game. Nothing was said about coach Marv Levy's decision to have the league's best offense repeatedly punt on fourth-and-short. Blame had been shifted to the players, which is where NFL coaches want the blame.

On the rare occasion when TV announcers behold an NFL coach going for it rather than doing the "safe" thing, to a man announcers say: "He's taking a huge gamble!" Actually, he's playing the percentages, since not punting on fourth-and-short increases the likelihood of victory. This has been documented in extraordinary detail by Brian Burke, a stats-cruncher who founded the Web site Advanced Football Analytics.

In 2005, I asked Don Shula, Hall of Fame coach who ran the Dolphins' 1972 perfect team, if there was any major football innovation waiting to be tried. His eyes twinkled. Shula said, "Someday there will be a coach who doesn't punt."

Later, I heard from an Arkansas referee who told me he'd worked games at a high school whose coach never sent out the punt unit. The school is Pulaski Academy of Little Rock, coached by Kevin Kelley. On average, NFL teams punt five times per game; on average, Kelley teams punt once per season. Here are recent results for Pulaski Academy:

2009—punted twice, reached state semifinals.
2010—did not punt, reached state championship.
2011—punted once, won state championship.
2012—did not punt, reached state semifinals.
2013—punted three times, reached state quarterfinals.
2014—did not punt, won state championship.

Six seasons, six punts, six playoff appearances, two state championships. The punts came when Pulaski was so far ahead the Bruins wanted to give the ball back, to avoid running up the score.

Prep football is different from the NFL on many points, including the strength of punters' legs. But Kelley's basic reasoning applies at any level of the sport:

"Everyone says it's a game of field position but it is not, it's a game of scoring and turnovers. Turnovers are the number-one stat in football, a much better predictor of victory than field position. Yet coaches in the NFL, the highest paid in the profession, coach for field position. Seeking field position, they punt the ball away—essentially awarding a turnover to the other team.

"Going for it on fourth down inevitably means sometimes you fail and send your defense out in a bad situation. But it also means most of the time you keep the ball and do not send your defense out at all. The defensive players and coaches need to understand this dynamic. Also, it helps if your home crowd understands so they won't boo after a failed fourth-down attempt. The first few times we went for it on fourth-and-long, our own crowd booed. Now when I keep the offense on the field on fourth-and-long, the crowd cheers.

"In addition to helping you maintain possession, knowing you won't punt opens up your playcalling. In the NFL, if it's third-and-6 then you have to gain at least six yards because you're going to punt on fourth-and-1. That dictates pass: the defense can send out its dime because they know the offense will throw. If you've already decided not to punt, then third-

and-6 is like second-and-6. You can call anything in the play-book; the defense can't situation-substitute because they don't know what's coming. There's a lot more flexibility if you call plays on third down knowing that you're going on fourth down. And basically you are giving yourself 33 percent more plays.

"But coaches don't want to make high-pressure decisions and be criticized. If you punt, it's a nonevent. No one remembers. If you go for it, everyone remembers. A lot of coaches would prefer that their decisions not be remembered, that only the athletes' successes or failures be remembered. Think about Belichick's call against the Colts. There has been more comment on that play than on all the punts in similar situations that led to defeat for the punting team.

"People in the pros have heard about my philosophy and talked to me about it. One NFL coach told me, 'You're right but if I try this and don't win, I will be fired along with all my assistants. If I play by traditional tactics and lose, I keep my job.'"

Beyond Kelley's views, there is an argument that even if the try fails, going for it on fourth down is better than punting. Going for it tells the players their coach is challenging them to win; launching a punt tells the players their coach is trying not to lose.

In the 2008 AFC championship game, San Diego trailed New England by 9 points—that's two scores—midway through the fourth quarter. The Chargers faced fourth down on the Patriots' 36, and head coach Norv Turner sent out the punt unit. It's a playoff game, there is no tomorrow! San Diego punted *in opposition territory in the fourth quarter when trailing in a playoff game!* Disgusted, the football gods saw to it that San Diego never touched the ball again. By punting, Turner told his players, "I've quit on this game so you might as well quit too." Going for it would have sent the opposite message.[*]

Economists assume all men and women are rational actors, little Mr. Spocks who always do whatever is logical. NFL coaches are not rational about punting on fourth-and-short. Not, that is, if the goal is victory for the team. If the coach is more concerned with his own job tenure than with seeking a win, then fraidy-cat punting is quite rational.

---

[*] Who cares if it was fourth-and-10? Who cares if it was fourth-and-99? San Diego's choices at that juncture were to try for the first down, or lose.

# Maybe You're Not Reading Enough Football Poetry

Once on the NPR program *All Things Considered*, host Robert Siegel, possessed of human history's best radio voice, said in that voice, "Gregg Easterbrook has the genre of humorous football poetry pretty much locked up." A small genre—in fact, microscopic. But mine. Here is a light haiku for each of the NFL's thirty-two teams.

## NFC EAST

First team with bombshell
cheerleaders; trophies nice too.
The Dallas Cowboys.

Set, hut, Hacksensack:
"Somewhere in swamps of Jersey."
New Jersey Giants.

Runs the Blur Offense:
Snap! Snap! Snap! Snap! Snap! (Gasp.) Snap!
The Philly Eagles.

Practice in VA,
perform in MD. Call selves
"Washington" franchise?

## AFC EAST

It's up! And…wide right.
In Super Bowl, woe-for-four.
The Buffalo Bills.

None can ever take
away seventeen and zed.
Miami Dolphins.

Since Bachelors III
all downhill for the green-clad.
The New Jersey Jets.

Glam-boy quarterback,
cold-fish coach: the combo works.
N.E. Patriots.

## NFC NORTH

Frigid wind off lake,
sleet, snow. Then weather gets bad.
Chicago's Da Bears.

No one will ever
take away zed and sixteen.
The Detroit Lions.

Fans have the common
sense to wear fake cheese on heads.
The Green Bay Packers.

They, Bills lost all four
S. Bowls. If met, one would have
to win. The Vikings.

## AFC NORTH

Only manly men
can wear purple uniforms.
Bal-a-mer Ravens.

Bush 41 was
prez when last postseason win.
The Cincy Bengals.

Fifty-one years since
a title. But who's counting?
Browns (2.0).

Steel industry yields
to software. Football changeless.
The Pittsburgh Steelers.

## NFC SOUTH

Rise up! Rise up and
defraud Georgia taxpayers!
Atlanta Falcons.

Better than Dillon
Panthers? Will never find out.
Carolina Cats.

Logo says Boy Scouts.
Style of play says otherwise.
The New Orleans Saints.

Drop videogame
jerseys, bring back Creamsicle.
Tampa Buccaneers.

## AFC SOUTH

Manning out, Luck in:
Interchangeable parts at
QB. Indy Colts.

In little brother
relationship to Cowboys.
The Houston Texans.

Feline endangered
across U.S. Extinct in
Florida. Jaguars.

Check logo: this team
should be called Flaming Thumbtacks.
Tennessee Titans.

## NFC WEST

Call them Cactus Wrens:
They, not cards, are the state bird.
AZ Cardinals.

Left Los Angeles
for a new place to complain.
The (question mark) Rams.

So long San Fran: now
make home 40 miles to south.
Santa Clara team.

Just hand off! Just hand
off! Just hand off! Just—oh, no.
Seattle Seahawks.

## AFC WEST

Have cheerleaders who
chant, *Giddyup! Giddyup!*
The Denver Broncos.

Eighty thousand in
red: visible from orbit.
Kansas City Chiefs.

Wanders the state of
California seeking home.
The (Oakland?) Raiders.

Dude, let's hit the beach.
Whoa, we have a game today?
San Diego Bolts.

# Predict NFL Winners Without Even Knowing Who's Playing

In a moment I will reveal a surefire, battle-tested, all-weather formula that anyone can use to dominate workplace NFL pools. Year in, year out my formula bests the experts. Those Vegas betting services with their 800 numbers? Keep your money in your wallet, because I am about to give my secret away.

First, a few words on the nonsense of predicting NFL outcomes to begin with.

Sportswriters need to fill space and sportscasters need to fill airtime: still, trying to predict game outcomes, or preseason predictions of who will make the postseason, are a fool's errand. The week before the 2014 season, for instance, *Sports Illustrated* predicted the Tampa Bay Buccaneers would win their division. They finished 2–14, the league's worst record.

Predictions about practically everything are wrong, and I don't just mean talking heads dashing off wild guesses regarding elections or the Dow Jones. Consider some prophecies from the highly credentialed. In 2006, the National Center for

Atmospheric Research predicted with "98 percent confidence" that the next solar cycle would be extremely strong; instead the cycle was the weakest in a century. In 2010, Treasury Secretary Timothy Geithner said there was "no possibility" U.S. debt issues would lose their AAA rating. One year later, they lost that rating.[*] The hilarious 1998 book *The Experts Speak*, by Christopher Cerf and Victor Navasky, is 445 pages of predictions that sailed wide of the mark. For instance, in 1959, Paul Samuelson, among the world's leading economists, forecast the Soviet economy would overtake the United States economy by the 1980s. Today, the United States GDP is 9.5 times that of the Russian Federation.

As regards football, the nuttiest exercise is attempting to predict exact final scores.

A decade ago, I published an incredibly scientifically advanced calculation, done on the back of a cocktail napkin, concluding there was a 1–in–500 chance of predicting an exact NFL final score, if confining predictions to the band of probable score outcomes.

My incredibly advanced calculation was testable, because the *New York Times* then ran weekly exact final score predictions while Scripps-Howard News Service then rang up dozens of A-, B-, and C-list celebs to ask their exact final score predictions for the Super Bowl.[†] I tracked the *Times* and Scripps-Howard final score predictions for several years. Cumulatively, they

---

[*] Perhaps we should worry that, in 2012, former Federal Reserve Chair Alan Greenspan said there is "zero possibility" the United States will default.

[†] Lamentably, Scripps-Howard, founded in 1917, folded in 2013, pulling up just shy of a century of reporting the news.

went 5-for-3,026—five predictions right against 3,021 wrong. Given this miserable track record, forecasting final scores seems sheer futility. Though note the result was nearly spot-on: a 1-in-500 chance. I correctly predicted the ability to predict!

If you must forecast final scores, at least don't foresee unlikely outcomes, especially final scores involving a team recording 2, 4, 5, 8, 11, 15, 18, 19, 22, 29, 36, 39, or 43 total points, or any number above 45. These score totals just don't occur much in football, so putting one into a final score prediction is asking for trouble. The new 2015 rule encouraging deuce tries after a touchdown may bring some traditionally unlikely final scores into fashion. But pair two of these numbers and you're sure to be wrong. I paired a few unlikely outcomes to check, and found that, going into the 2015 season, there had never been an NFL final score of 43–18, 39–19, 38–11, 18–11 or 11–5.*

For the 2011 NFL divisionals round, the *Wall Street Journal* forecast final scores of Steelers over Ravens 22–18 and Packers over Falcons 26–25. These predictions were wrong, as you've surmised: double-down wrong, since there has never been an NFL final score of 22–18 or of 26–25. Though 2–0 occurred five times, most recently in 1938, before rules were changed to enliven offense. Considering the fifth quarter was instituted in 1940, no NFL contest has ended 2–0 in overtime. Attending a game that ends 2–0 in overtime is on my bucket list.

Not only do "experts" engage in the futility of attempting to predict exact final scores, some predict outcomes that are

---

* I did not check for finals involving one side above 45 points, since there would be lots of never-happened outcomes in the format (45+X)-N, where N is any final score.

impossible. One week in 2014, Fox Sports forecast that the Saints would defeat the 49ers 27.6–25.2, while the Bengals would best the Browns by 22.9 to 19. The latter prediction combined bêtes noires—one score that is impossible with another that is improbable. In statistics, students learn the fallacy of adding up estimates, dividing, then treating the result as more precise than any of the estimates. The sports world slept late the day that was covered in class.

Word to the wise: always predict an NFL game ends 20–17. This is the most common final score, occurring three times in the 2014 season, forty-four times in the last decade, and 245 times in league history. The second-most common final score is 17–10, occurring twenty-four times in the last decade and 132 times in league annals.[*] If you perpetually forecast that every NFL game of the season would end 20–17, you'd be right at least occasionally, and look like a genius compared to "experts" who spend hours breaking down film and charting tendencies.

And now the surefire success secret for forecasting NFL results. Employ this simple formulation: **Best record wins; if records equal, home team wins.**

Using this formula, you don't need to pore over stats or access proprietary algorithms. You don't need to know how Team A's quarterback does throwing to his left when the barometric pressure is rising or Team B's average gain allowed against the weak side screen on second-and-long. You don't need whispered insider information.

You don't need to expend valuable time thinking. You don't

---

[*] I am indebted to the sorting tool Pro-Football-Reference.com, which enabled me to determine the obscure information in this paragraph.

even need to know who's playing! Just pick the team with the best record, or if records are equal, pick the home team.

For the 2014 season, the surefire success secret went 191–75–1. With 191 outcomes correctly forecast,* the surefire secret was right 72 percent of the time.

How does this compare to the experts? For 2014, ESPN published fourteen sets of expert predictions: from Mike Ditka, Mike Golic, Ron Jaworski, Keyshawn Johnson, Chris Mortenson, Adam Schefter and others who do nothing year-round but talk football. The best ESPN predictor, Tom Jackson, called 183 outcomes correctly—none too shabby, but less than the 191 correct from my generic off-price formula. Schefter was right 173 times, Mortensen correct 164 times: both specialize in claims of possessing exclusive insider information, and both did notably worse than plugging really basic public info into a simple rule. With 160 correct, Ditka barely got above using an even simpler rule, always choosing the home team: the home team being victorious 152 times in the 2014 season.

Over the last decade the surefire formula—best record wins; if records equal, home team wins—has outperformed the experts every season except 2013. If experts would stop thinking and follow this automated formula, they'd look smarter. Anyway, it can work for you.

This formula is for straight-up predictions, not against the spread. I've compared outcomes to ESPN's straight-up predictions.

---

* The Seattle-New England Super Bowl was a neutral site meeting of teams of identical won-loss standing. The Seahawks were the home team of record, so I counted that contest as a loss for my formula.

The straight-up result, win or lose, is what counts in the standings. Beyond that, the spread matters only to gamblers: the downside of gambling is noted in Chapter four. My compromise with my Baptist upbringing is to like girls and dancing but oppose gambling. No one cares how much the Donald Trumps of the world lose at the casino. For most people, gambling only brings sorrow—sometimes, destroys families. This renders me allergic to the spread, which is a mechanism for causing average people to throw away money. Don't make big bets: the house always wins.

But for those who participate in harmless $10 workplace NFL pools, here's a wagering tip. The NFL playoff format is wild cards, divisionals, conference titles, Super Bowl. Take the home teams in the divisional round. They are the surest sure-thing in sports.

Since the current NFL postseason format was adopted in 1990, home teams in the divisional round are 73–27, a 73 percent winning figure. That's well north of the 57 percent rate at which NFL home teams won in 2014 regular season contests.

For the divisional round, the reason the hosts are hosting is that they are the best teams. Equally important, host clubs have spent a bye week relaxing in hot tubs while their opponents were out in the cold being pounded. NFL teams with an extra week to relax and prepare consistently outperform teams that played the previous week—and in the divisional round, all the home teams had an extra week.

So in the divisional round, bet on the home teams in your NFL workplace or school pool. You don't even need to know who's playing!

A week later, in the championship round, homefield advantage dissipates. Since 1990, hosts in conference championship games are 31–19, a 62 percent winning figure, only a little above the rate at which hosts win regular season games. For the championship round, nobody's had the previous week off and the Super Bowl is just one W away. Players leave everything on the field in championship contests, meaning home teams won't necessarily be the favorites. But in the divisional round, look homeward.

Caveat: All Predictions Wrong or Your Money Back.

# Iron Laws of the Gridiron

Over years of watching and attending too many football games, then writing about them for ESPN, the *New York Times*, *The Atlantic* and NFL.com, I have observed a few iron laws of the sport:

**The Law of Fourth Down Courage:** If the other team is relieved to see your kicking team trotting onto the field, then you ought to be going for it. *When the TV announcer says, "It's fourth down, the Screaming Lemurs have to kick"—no, they don't. But that's surely what the opponent is hoping for.*

**The Law of the Goal Line:** Use play-fakes from a jumbo set, sprint-outs or just run the ball—whatever you do, don't call a regular pass pattern from a regular formation. *In other words, don't do what the Seahawks did at the end of the 2015 Super Bowl. Yours truly wrote in 2001, "When you get to the goal line you must not throw regular passes from regular passing sets. Regular passes don't work at the goal line because the closer the offense comes to the goal line, the less territory the defense must protect. By the time the offense reaches the opponent's 1-yard line, it is nearly impossible for a receiver to get open on a regular pattern."*

**The Law of When to Throw at the Goal Line:** If you're going to throw at the goal line, do it on first and goal, with the defense cranked to stop a rush, not on second and goal, after the defense just stuffed a rush. *Reaching the goal line at the end of the 2015 Super Bowl, the Seahawks ran on first down, then threw on second down, the reverse of optimal strategy.*

**The Law of Short Yardage:** Do a little dance if you want to gain that yard. Successful short-yardage plays must involve a shift or misdirection, so the defense has an instant of confusion just before the snap. *Seattle's final Super Bowl play lacked this, too.*

**The Law of the Blitz:** Good quarterbacks want to be blitzed—please don't throw me into that briar patch!—because this ensures single coverage downfield. *Only two of the last ten Super Bowls were won by teams that blitzed more than average, the Steelers in 2006 and 2009. Generally, the best teams employ orthodox defense.*

**The Law of Sacks:** Fans and TV announcers go wild for sacks, but in contemporary football the clang of incompletions is the essence of defense. *It's been five years since the team that led the NFL in sacks won a postseason game that same season. Three of the NFL's five most recent league-leading sack artists were on teams that did not reach the postseason. Incompletions and pressures—forcing the quarterback to throw the ball away—have more to do with victory than sacks.*

**The Law of Defensive Passing Stats:** Bad teams have impressive pass-defense stats because their opponents attain big leads, then work the clock by keeping the ball on the ground. *In 2014, the Bills, Browns, Chargers, Chiefs, Dolphins, 49ers and*

*Vikings posted great pass-defense stats—and none reached the postseason.*

**The Law of Offensive Passing Stats:** Yards per attempt is the important offensive metric in contemporary football. *In the 2014 season, six of the top seven teams for yards per attempt made the playoffs.*

**The Law of Comebacks:** Defense starts comebacks, offense stops them. *Teams that fall behind need to focus on defense; teams trying to thwart a comeback need to focus on offense.*

**The Law of Sportsmanship:** When the winner runs up the score, the victor, not the vanquished, should feel embarrassed. *Only chumps and punks boast about how much they won by.*

**The Law of the Front Five:** The least recognizable players in football, offensive linemen are the soul of the sport. *If you could choose between a team with a great quarterback and an average offensive line, or an average quarterback and a great offensive line, you'd be crazy not to take the latter.*

**The Law of Going All-Out:** Victories don't come in the mail, seize the day! *Trying to win is always better than trying not to lose.*

**The Law of the Reverse:** Any reverse that gets back to the line of scrimmage is a plus for the offense, because it forces the defense to "stay home," playing a hesitant style. Because of this, every game plan should include a reverse. *King Arthur will return from Avalon sooner than TV announcers learn the difference between an end-around, a reverse and a double reverse.*

**The Law of Conservation of Timeouts:** In most cases, just take a five-yard delay-of-game penalty, because saving the time out is more important. *But then use your conserved timeouts!*

*Many coaches make puzzling clock-management decisions late in the half, as if unused timeouts can be donated to charity.*

**The Law of the Onside:** The surprise onside kickoff is football's most underused tactic. *A surprise onside wagers a turnover for your team against about 25 yards of field position for the opponent—and that's a good wager.*

**The Law of Possession Being Nine-Tenths of the Law:** Possession of the football is worth far more than field position. *This is the reason NFL coaches should order more onside kicks and fourth-and-short tries.*

**The Law of Gatorade Showers:** Do not pour the bucket over the coach's head unless you've won a championship. *The trend of Gatorade showers for routine regular season contests highlights the fact that the team in question hasn't done anything yet.*

**The Law of Double-Naughts:** Never celebrate until the clock shows 00. *Celebrating early is like asking the football gods to smite thee down. And trust me, you don't want to be smote.*

**The Law of Authentic Celebrations:** Touchdowns are fun and exciting, players should be allowed to dance around and celebrate. *The dumbest rule in football—robotically enforced at the high school, college, and pro levels—is the 15-yard penalty for jumping up and down after a score.*

**The Law of Faux Celebrations:** Do not wildly celebrate a routine tackle or short pass. Don't give a theatrical "first down!" signal after gaining 6 yards with your team trailing by 20 points. Celebrate only touchdowns, turnovers and the double-naughts. *In 2014, Detroit Lions linebacker Stephen Tulloch leapt into the air to celebrate a mundane tackle in an early-season game. He injured his knee and couldn't play again that year.*

**The Law of Weasels:** When you hire a coach who's only in it for himself, you get a coach who's only in it for himself. *Football teams hire away each other's coaches, thinking someone who just broke his last set of promises will become an honest man who keeps his current promises.*

**The Law of Data-Driven Mush:** "Data-driven" is the #1 buzz phrase of current sports commentary, but often all it really tells you is that winning teams have better statistics than losing teams.

**The Iron Law of the Pick-Six:** Return an interception for a touchdown, win the Super Bowl. *Really, it's that simple. Teams that run an interception back to the house are 12-0 in the ultimate contest.*

# Football Maxims to Live By

Most football locker rooms are plastered with posters of cheesy inspirational sayings printed over scenes of mountain climbing. But don't think you can't learn from self-help sentimentality. Here are three locker room sayings that all should take to heart:

**There is only one thing in life you can control—yourself.** You can't control what other people do and you certainly can't control what they think of you. You cannot control whether your luck is good or bad. But you can control yourself.

**There are no shortcuts to any place worth going.** Ice cream provides instant gratification. Everything else requires effort.

**It's not whether you get knocked down, it's whether you get back up.** This Vince Lombardi quotation is the number-one increment of sports wisdom with broad life applicability. Lombardi may have been a grouchy old coot. But he was sure right about this.

And here are life lessons encoded in football:

**Keep your eye off the ball.** Ninety percent of what's important happens away from the focus of attention.

**Don't panic now, there will be plenty of time for that later.** Suppose you fall behind early in a football game—what's the point of panicking? In nearly all life situations, getting upset only makes things worse. Keep trying, and the situation may change.

**Life is a team sport.** In football the quarterback gets too much credit for wins, too much blame for losses. The same obtains in many organizations—excessive praise or criticism for presidents, CEOs, directors, chairs. The accomplishments or disappointments of any organization are attributable to its performance as a team.

**The coach who yells is wasting everyone's time, including his own.** In athletics, business, academics, community affairs and the family, effective leaders are ones who challenge others to improve, rather than denigrating. Anger and yelling are signs of lack of leadership.

**Let competition make you strong but never hostile.** Wishing ill to your opponent, whether in athletics, the workplace, romance or any other pursuit, indicates poor character and will come back to haunt you.

**Root for whoever defeated you.** Good sportsmanship dictates that if Team A defeats Team B fair and square, Team B should root for Team A to win the championship. This standard applies broadly to life. Don't be bitter about someone who gets ahead of you at work, school or romance. Root for that person to do well. The good vibes created will come back to you someday, somehow.

**Always have something in your pocket.** Football coaches don't necessarily call their best plays—they may keep a good play in their pocket, just in case. In many aspects of life, holding something in reserve can help.

**'Ere the clock strikes midnight, head back to your house/apartment/hotel/friend's place.** Crimes, arrests and traffic deaths spike between midnight and dawn. Smart coaches teach athletes to avoid being out during this period. Unless you work a graveyard shift, being home between midnight and dawn is a good rule.

**Even if it seems like the whole world is cheating, don't.** There have always been cheaters. There always will be. You are better than that.

**Save the best for last.** One reason the NFL has endured multiple scandals yet thrived is that in many years the season's final game, the Super Bowl, has been the season's best game. This leaves a sweet aftertaste. Well-run entertainment organizations save the best for last. It's a good rule in almost any area of life.

**We're all day-to-day.** Injured athletes may be described as "day-to-day." Each morning, remind yourself that you and everyone you care about are always day-to-day.

# Index

# Index

*Index*

Namath, Joe, 1–2, 11
narcotic painkillers, 153n
National Basketball Association, 28, 58, 63, 145
National Domestic Violence Hotline, 84
National Federation of High Schools, 41, 100n, 146
National Football League (NFL)
African Americans and, 16, 122–123, 166–167
American Football League merger with, 157
American mania for, xiii
attendance, 17, 55
broadcast partners of, 76–77
in Canada, 140–141
commissioned report on New England Patriots, ix
community and, xvi
concussions in, 103n
contracts, 53n
corporate welfare received by, 131
as cult, 11–12
DirecTV and, 140–142
draft, 74, 149, 149n
enthusiasm for, xvi
in European Union, 61
expansion of, 60–65
fantasy package, 117–118, 121
finances of, 56–57
future of, 143–145
Heidi Game, 3–6, 158
hidden costs, 132
idolizing, 117–118
lawsuits against, 40n
live-streaming, 30, 64–65
logo, 30n
in Mexico, 62, 140–141
as mirror of American society, xiii–xiv, 8–13, 84, 154–155
NLL and, 115

as outlet for emotions, xv
owners, 14, 57n, 58, 75n, 76, 129, 130, 134, 135, 142
popularity of, 115, 118–119, 121, 144
predicting outcomes in, 193–199
problems of, xvi
ratings, xiii, 55–56, 119
reforms, 149–155
revenue, xv, 57, 131
rosters, 11
special treatment of, xv, 133
strikes, 17
structure of, 8
taxes and, 132
television and, xiii, 27–28, 30
typical career in, 11
women and, xiv
*See also* stadiums; subsidies; Super Bowl; taxpayers; USA Football
National High School Sports Related Injury Surveillance Study, 103
NBC (network), xiii, 3–6, 29, 31, 70–71, 73, 131, 158
NCAA. *See* college football
Neely, Ralph, 37
neurological damage, 100–103, 104n, 106, 116, 151
*Neurology*, 102
New England Patriots
Buffalo Bill against, 174
helmet logo of, 14n
illegal tapes of, xii, 13, 13n, 169
Indianapolis Colts against, ix–x, 168, 178
Los Angeles Rams against, 167
New York Giants against, 169–170
NFL-commissioned report on, ix
offense, 45n
passing of, 49

**Gregg Easterbrook** is the author of ten books, including *The King of Sports, The Progress Paradox, The Leading Indicators* and *Sonic Boom*. He is a contributing editor of the *Atlantic* and the *Washington Monthly* and a former columnist for ESPN.com. He has been a distinguished fellow of the Fulbright Foundation, a visiting fellow of the Brookings Institution and a political columnist for Reuters.